D1638971

THE
Archive Photographs
SERIES

WARRINGTON
RAILWAYS

RE-BUILDING OF BANK QUAY, 1961. Looking north in February, it is obvious that the removal of the canopy glazing has created a bright and open atmosphere where once dark and gloom ruled. The train being whistled away is from London to Blackpool; today passengers would have to change at Preston. While this practise still exists, much of this scene is from another world. The uniforms and general clutter have gone, as have the LNWR style wooden buildings. Great attempts now have to be made to keep stations litter free.

THE
Archive Photographs
SERIES

WARRINGTON
RAILWAYS

Compiled by
Bob Pixton

CHALFORD

The Chalford Publishing Company
St Mary's Mill, Chalford,
Stroud, Gloucestershire, GL6 8NX

ISBN 0 7524 0750 3

Typesetting and origination by
The Chalford Publishing Company
Printed in Great Britain by
Redwood Books, Trowbridge

Front cover illustration
Approaching Warrington from the south is one of Stanier's ubiquitous Black Fives
in steam's final hours during the 1960s.

BANK QUAY, LOW LEVEL, 1950s. And people wonder why rail travel isn't preferred to cars! Looking west on a sunny day, this picture shows the two platforms for Manchester (London Road) and Widnes and Liverpool (Lime Street) in the dark and gloom.

Contents

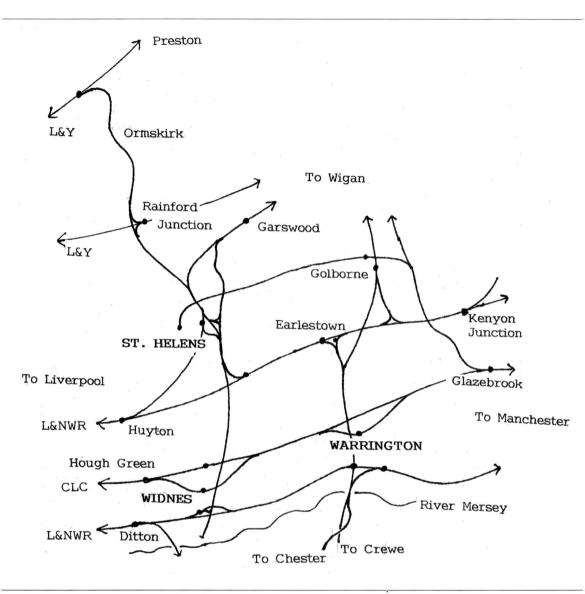

WARINGTON'S RAIL NETWORK, 1922. The main line railway scene of South Lancashire is dominated by the north-south main Anglo-Scottish route and the four, almost east-west parallel routes, between the two largest cities. Warrington figures heavily in all compass directions.

Introduction

With Warrington being the highest crossing point of the River Mersey, it was natural for industry to develop there. Equally understandable was the desire to construct lines from north to south and later, from west to east in order to connect these industries with their market places and suppliers of raw materials. The Liverpool and Manchester Railway induced several independent lines to run from it; typical of these was the line north from Warrington to Newton in 1831. At the same time collieries in the Haydock area linked up with these lines, thereby allowing their products to travel at speeds, and in quantities, previously only dreamed of.

The development of the Grand Junction Railway from the south, together with others, became the London and North Western Railway making today's west coast main line to Scotland. The first east-west line through the town was part of the St Helens' Canal and Railway Company and Warrington and Stockport Railway's end-to-end ventures that linked (Manchester) Altincham to Garston Docks and Liverpool. Subsequently, the Cheshire Lines Committee built a connection between Cressington, in Liverpool, to Trafford Park, in Manchester, because they were fed up with being held to ransom by other companies' lines. This forms the current line through Central Station.

KENYON JUNCTION, 1960. Porter and booking clerk, Sid Ball, douses the gas lights for the last time on Saturday 31 December when the station closed.

VULCAN PRODUCT, 1961. 'The old order meets the new'. Fifteen Type AL3, 25kV AC electric Bo-Bo locos were built in 1960/61. After the loading gauge is checked in Vulcan Siding, Stanier 8F 2-8-0 No. 48722 collects brand new No. E3098 in March.

By the time the last line locally opened in 1900, the face of South Lancashire had changed out of all recognition. Numerous industries had set up in the major towns, taking advantage of the easily available fuel, docks and an excellent transport system. It would take the decline in coal production, followed by the rapid, relentless availability of motor transport to decimate the local passenger services and the goods trains. The widespread distribution of North Sea gas also contributed to the decline of facilities at local stations.

Lack of investment means that limited encouragement exists to improve the system. Local authorities are having to play a bigger role in transportation but their budgets are restricted. So what of the future? Will privatisation bring about a much needed renaissance, or the complete demise of the railway system? Who knows?

Bob Pixton
Swindon
October 1996

One

Over the Water to Warrington

The line north of Warrington was opened on 25 July 1831 by the Warrington and Newton Railway. It went from a westerly curve at Newton Junction and split into two at Warrington. One branch went to the passenger terminus at Dallum Lane, the other, serving local industries, ended north of the Liverpool turnpike road. The easterly curve at Newton Junction was built in 1837. With the development of the Grand Junction Railway to Birmingham, which opened on 4 July 1837, Dallum Lane closed and a through station was opened south of the Liverpool Road. This station closed just over thirty years later, to be replaced by Bank Quay a little further south, on top of the Garston-Altrincham line. South of Warrington the main line went to Crewe and, from 1857, a joint line (GW and LNWR) to Chester. The former met the line from Liverpool at Weaver Junction.

WARRINGTON, DOWN FAST, 1940. Waiting to leave northwards is Blue Coronation Class Pacific No. 6224 *Princess Alexandra*. These engines, with their streamlined shape and white speed lines, must have caused a few heads to turn. Of particular interest are the LNWR signals, especially the tall repeater in front of the engine and the diminutive ground signals in-between the lines.

MOORE TROUGHS, 1959. Before 1876, trains to and from the north stopped at Warrington to pick up water. As this lengthened the journey time it is not surprising that the LNWR authorised a set of troughs at Moore, some two miles south. This was a flat piece of line, on a gentle curve with slight rising gradients at each end. Three real problems existed with this method of trains taking on water. Areas of hard water needed special treatment to stop the boiler tubes from furring up more quickly than they would normally do. The water needed to be ice free in winter which meant heating and, as this picture demonstrates, spillages occurred. These not only caused a degree (!) of passenger discomfort, but also tended to wash away the ballast, necessitating extra maintenance. The pumping station is the tall building to the right, Moore station was just north of it. This line side shot shows the 11.15 Blackpool North-Crewe on 8 August 1959, hauled by an unidentified Hughes-Fowler Crab 2-6-0. The fireman has been too slow in winding back up the scoop. Consequently, too much water has passed into the tender causing it to overflow, in dramatic fashion.

ACTON GRANGE. Just south of Warrington, the main line crosses firstly, the River Mersey, and then, from 1893, the Manchester Ship Canal. South of the latter the Crewe and Chester lines diverge from Acton Grange Junction. Before the canal was built, the line was at a lower level on the right. To cross the canal, embankments were created and the line rose at a gradient of 1 in 130. The bridge over the canal is in the distance and, hidden against the iron work, is the controlling signal box.

ACTON GRANGE, 1959. Viewed from the other side of the bridge can be seen Jubilee Class 4-6-0 No. 45633 *Aden* with a train from Crewe to Warrington. The engine was built at Crewe twenty-five years before. Barely discernible on the left are the abutments for another bridge. This was over the 'old' line before the MSC was built.

ACTON GRANGE, 1964. Passing along the line to Crewe in July, was Jubilee Class 4-6-0 No. 45698 *Mars* with a mixed freight train. The yellow diagonal stripe on the cab side was to remind the foot plate crew that the engine was banned from the line south of Crewe, where the overhead wires were. This 1936 Crewe built engine lasted until October 1965. The tender it entered service with actually belonged to Royal Scot Class No. 6166, *Mars* getting the smaller Midland Fowler tender. This was replaced by that of Patriot class No. 5545 during the rebuilding of the class between 1946 and 1949.

DARESBURY, 1962. Although just under three miles from Warrington, the extent of the associated works for the Manchester Ship Canal was felt here. The 'old' line is to the left of the picture with the deviated line on the right. Standard Class 5 4-6-0 No. 73039 is coming down the gradient with a train to Bangor from Manchester. The old lines were used for wagon storage, or as places of refuge for slower moving freight trains for over seventy years after the canal was cut.

ACTON GRANGE SIGNAL BOX, 1969. Many of the signal boxes along the main line were rebuilt, in the 1940s, in this Air Raid Precaution design of H.E. Morgan. The walls were fourteen inches thick and the floor and roof were of reinforced concrete: all designed to withstand bomb blast or a smaller, direct hit. This one, unlike others of its type, had windows on both sides and an external stair case. This view was taken from a southbound train on the Chester line.

ACTON GRANGE JUNCTION, 1963. Coming up the gradient along the Chester line is Class 5 4-6-0 No. 45069 on 17 August, heading towards Warrington. On the left is part of tunnel No. 75. During the construction of the MSC, the LNWR wanted to keep the old and new lines as insurance in case the compensation for their deviation was lengthy. It would only need a landslip on the new embankment to prompt their rivals to start a new race to the north. High rail charges were the reason for the canal's construction. The transport charge for one ton of cheese from Liverpool to Manchester was quoted as 10s; it would only cost 15s to transport it 3,000 miles across the Atlantic.

ACTON GRANGE JUNCTION, 1904. This view, taken from the south bank, looks west along the Manchester Ship Canal. The old main line used to occupy the land close to the embankment. To the north was Walton (Old) Junction and the bridge over the River Mersey. The lines were elevated and deviated over the canal, opening in 1893. The signal box was built to span the lines to give maximum visibility and would be replaced in 1940 by the ARP box, a short distance to the south. Under the bridge can be seen wagons on the lines serving the ship canal, passing under the main lines by the bridge on the right.

HAYDOCK WHARF, 1963. Haydock Collieries had wharves for unloading foreign grown pit props from the ship canal. The National Coal Board had their own shunters for the work, one of which was 0-6-0T *Haydock*, seen here in September 1963. In the early days of coal mining it was quite common for company trains and engines to pass over main lines to Liverpool and other towns and cities. After a BR check, this engine went via Bank Quay, along the WCML to Earlestown to get back onto NCB metals.

WALTON OLD JUNCTION, 1961. Stanier 8F No. 48259 is just crossing the River Mersey on the original Twelve Arches. This was the path of the Grand Junction Railway in the early days. Of the three routes it could have taken, it will ascend the link up to the main line and pass through Bank Quay Station on its way to Carlisle. The middle signal was for Arpley Extension Sidings, while the left hand route was for Arpley Junction and the east. The 'new' main line is to the right and a sister 8F is heading south with a train of empty Covhops for Northwich.

WALTON NEW JUNCTION, 1968. To cross the River Mersey there are two bridges: carrying the original route of the main line are the Twelve Arches and, carrying the new main line, as from 1893, was a steel girder bridge at a higher level. South of these bridges the main line divides into the Crewe and Chester lines. Perched almost on top of the Mersey is this thirty lever frame box, which since 1948 has been on the west of the line. The scene in the background shows Crosfield's works and their transporter bridge across the river. As the bridge here is over a tidal part of a river, it needed Admiralty approval for safety. It was tested by driving two double headed trains, hauling loaded sand wagons, onto the centre of the bridge.

WALTON OLD JUNCTION, 1969. This box controlled lines to Arpley in the east and a new spur north, up at a gradient of 1 in 69, that met the main lines. The main line south went up to Acton Grange Junction. Lines south onto the MSC and Walton Old Sidings were also included in the box's thirty-eight levers. The box closed in 1972 with the electrification of the main line and the building of Warrington's Power Box.

Two
Bank Quay Station

The current Bank Quay Station is the third. For over a generation it was adjacent to the Liverpool Road Bridge before migrating 300 yards south on top of the east-west line from Manchester to Liverpool. A re-building project to accompany electrification completes the trio.

DOWN MAIN LINE, 1995. Roaring through the station at approximately 80 mph is preserved Standard Class 8 Pacific No. 71000 *Duke of Gloucester*. When built in 1954 it was intended to introduce a new era of efficient, reliable and easy to maintain express passenger locos. The building costs were just under £45,000 and it would have taken BR up to the expected electrification in the late 1970s. This largely experimental engine was visualised as an enlarged Britannia, with many features, such as the boiler barrel, in common. The Caprotti valve gear allowed a more free flow of steam and its rotary nature eliminated the wear in the motion pins and slides associated with normal valve gears. Consequently, thermal efficiency was constant between repairs and shed maintenance was also reduced. This valve gear was based upon results gleaned from twenty of Ivatt's LMS Black Five 4-6-0s. The name settled upon was the third choice, both *Prince Charles* and *Duke of Edinburgh* having been rejected. With the engine weighing in at 100 tons, its operational use was restricted. After covering just over a quarter of a million miles it was withdrawn in November 1962. A spell of eight years in scrapyards at Barry was followed by restoration and recommissioning by its namesake, in 1986.

WARRINGTON NO. 1 SIGNAL BOX, 1969. This large, typical LNWR type 5 brick box stood out, sentinel like, just beyond the south of Warrington Bank Quay Station. Behind it can be seen the marshalling yard adjacent to the line from Arpley. This view looks north to the station from the up main line. The signal gantry in the background controlled the passenger platform one and the up goods next to it. The height of the signal posts indicates the main use of that route, so that the passenger lines would be onto the 'up main' or the 'up Chester' while the goods' lines would be 'up Chester' or 'up main'. From the former there was a line down to the Arpley branch.

DOWN MAIN LINE, 1963. Racing through along the main line on 5 October is Coronation Class 4-6-2 No. 46251 *City of Nottingham* with an enthusiast's special. To the left can be seen box No.1, with its commanding view of the lines. To the rear of it are the sidings by the Arpley branch.

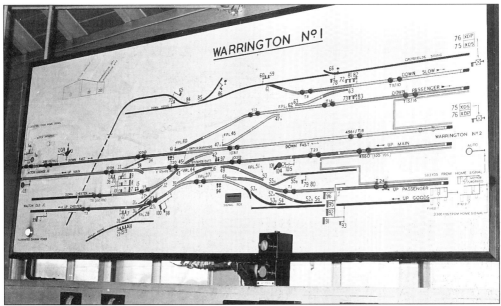

WARRINGTON NO.1 INTERIOR, 1972. The control panel of the signal box shows the main line from Acton Grange and Walton Old Junction, on the left, to the station, on the right. Signal boxes were built on such sites and at such heights to assist observations of passing trains. With the advent of track circuiting, the presence of a train could be detected by the small round lamps on the lines. In October the box would be replaced by a Power Signal Box (PSB), adjacent to the up end of the station, to go with the impending electrification.

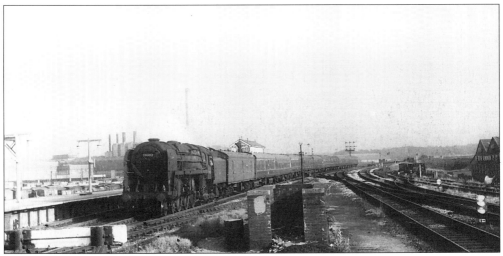

DOWN MAIN LINE, 1966. About to tear through the station is Britannia Class 4-6-2 No. 70002 *Geoffrey Chaucer* on the longest day with a north bound eleven coach train. To the right are the lines that serve the platform four and the down slow and, to the extreme right, is the rail connection to this part of the extensive Crosfield industrial complex. The three bracket signal post at the end of the train is for trains coming off of the Chester line. They could pass onto any of the three lines north.

DOWN FAST, 1964. Rebuilt Patriot 4-6-0 No. 45527 *Southport* storms through Bank Quay with a late summer express. Visible are the new double chimney and taper boiler which, together with the new cylinders, enabled these re-builds to be rated as 7P, one notch up. Above the engine dominating the sky-line is the building of Warrington Borough Council's redundant Electricity Generating Station. Although situated next to the railway, it received coal by barge and later, along a torturous conveyor belt system from Wilderspool Causeway.

UP MAIN LINE, 1967. Almost at the death throes of steam, seen here on 1 September is Britannia Class 4-6-2 No. 70035 *Rudyard Kipling* on relief train from Carlisle to Euston. Little had probably changed around the station for many years: the water column and brazier would have been recognisable items of station furniture a century earlier but the replacement of the gas lamps by concrete electric ones probably made at least one difference.

VIEW FROM WARRINGTON NO.1, 1972. On the extreme right is the new power signal box, with Lever's factory on the left. In the centre are the main lines with 80-85 mph speed restrictions. Waiting on the up goods line is a Class 37 signalled to pass onto the up Crewe line. The OHW give a very cluttered view.

BANK QUAY, 1957. Steaming through along the up main line on the last day of September is re-built Patriot 4-6-0 No. 45523 *Bangor*. The 1946 re-building process by Ivatt involved replacing the straight smoke deflectors, as well as other features, making these engines approximately ten per cent more powerful than the Fowler originals.

DOWN SLOW LINE, 1967. Creeping around the back of the station on the down goods line is Class 5 4-6-0 No. 45055. This was one of a batch of fifty engines built by nearby Vulcan Foundry between 1934 and 1935. It was withdrawn a year after this photograph. Gone are the semaphores; the diamond shape indicates that the signal is track circuited in the signal box (No. 2) and in the bay platform with a train to, probably, Liverpool. A two car DMU has replaced the steam hauled train of ten years before. It was from here that the push-pull service to St Helens departed. The factory to the right belongs to the Crosfield industries.

UP GOODS, 1964. Passing round the back of the station on the goods line is Standard class 9F 2-10-0 No. 92049 in June. No. 2 signal box is behind the engine with Crosfield's in the background. The wagons are from Parkside colliery and will have come from the L&M line at Earlestown. This is now the site of the car park for a DIY store.

BANK QUAY, 1966. An enthusiast's special has just come under Bank Quay Bridge and is leaving the up main line. The bridge carries the main road (A57) to Liverpool. In the later 1830s, to the north was a branch of the Warrington and Newton railway: to the south was the Grand Junction Railway. The turnpike road was elevated onto a bridge to enable the two lines to meet. Bank Quay Station was opened in 4 July 1837, south of the bridge. The terminus at Dallam Lane closed, although it continued to flourish as a goods line. Just over thirty years later the LNWR shifted Bank Quay Station a short distance south, opening it on 16 November 1868. The upheaval may not have seemed worthwhile except that the company's line from Altrincham to Ditton ran at a lower level so making a compact interchange station. The goods shed on the right became a diesel stabling point after Dallam's closure to steam in 1968. However, due to complaints from residents, the engines were transferred to their present day home at Arpley. The bridge was replaced by 1972 with one that allowed for greater clearance for the overhead wires.

BANK QUAY, 1966. Having pulled into platform one this train would go down the link to meet the branch from Arpley. Upon reversal it would call at the site of that station. Contrast the environment for passengers then with today's travellers, who simply wouldn't put up with being showered with clouds of steam, nor with the dirt that was implicit with a steam engine.

RAIL TOUR, 1957. While we think of such events as being relatively new and belonging to the end of steam era, this isn't true. The RCTS has been doing this for over fifty years: this one was around Warrington and District, in the lengthening sun's rays of October. LNER Class C13 4-4-2T No. 67436 and two non-corridor coaches, the first a celestory, conveyed men around a rail network largely unchanged since the turn of the century.

UP SLOW LINE, 1951. Shunting round the up side of the station is a member of the LNWR 5'
6" or 910 Class. It was one of 160 built from the1890s. Classified as 1P by the LMS is 2-4-2T
No. 46654 on 23 May. This is the second site of the hotel in the background, the original was
to the north and served as a booking office for the station there. It became a goods office upon
the opening of this station on 16 November 1868.

WARRINGTON PLATFORM TWO, 1964. About to pass through the station on the up main
line is Type 4 diesel electric No. D232. The LNWR signals have been replaced by upper
quadrant semaphores and ground discs. Bank Quay Station was enlarged in 1897 with new
signals and boxes. No. 2 box, with its eighty-two levers, was added in about 1925. While the
box is not as tall, nor as long as box No.1, it is of typical LNWR type 5 style.

BLACKPOOL TRAIN, 1960. The driver of Jubilee Class 4-6-0 No. 45584 *North West Frontier* seems to be very relaxed. This might suggest that rather than have a mad scramble to take on water at the adjacent LNWR column, the train made use of the Moore troughs, some two miles south. A reduction in the blast pipe diameter and an increase in superheater elements from 14 to 24, transformed their performance from 'indifferent' to 'competent'. A Stanier 8F is waiting on the up side of the station.

SHUNTING, 1960. Class Five 4-6-0 No. 44986 has just collected a 10 ton van from the adjacent sidings. It will add this to the front of its train before proceeding north. The engine was built at Horwich in 1946 and was fitted with a self weighing tender to allow various grades of coal to be assessed. To make way for the mechanism, the space for 250 gallons of water was sacrificed.

WARRINGTON SIGNAL BOXES NOS. 4 AND 5. The extensive railway connections to industry in the area necessitated much signalling. A few hundred yards north of No. 2 box was No. 4 box. This fifty odd lever box was slightly smaller than No. 2 box but recognisable as being from the same mould. Controlling events in the sidings only, was the smaller No. 5 box; the bridge is Frog Hall. As the photographs show, by 1969 rail-borne freight had declined to such a point that the connections to the sidings has been removed and the boxes were sliding down the vandalised slope to demolition.

LEAVING WARRINGTON, 1966. Emerging from the CLC over bridge along the down fast is Class 5 4-6-0 No. 45218 on 12 February. This Armstrong Whitworth engine was one of a batch of 100 built by them in 1935, at a cost of £5,119 each, including tender. Local industry was well served by both railway companies, hence the extensive sidings from the LNWR lines. The wagons on the left supplied industries from the CLC lines; the same factories, such as Pearson and Knowles, often had access to both railway companies

CLC BRIDGE. This is the same bridge but this time viewed from the south. When the lines were enlarged north of the station, only the under slung girder bridge central span had tracks through it. The 1888 map shows that forethought had been used, since brick arches were in place; later they were to take sidings, as this 1960s photograph shows. The photographer stood where the line from the goods warehouse on the up side, trailed into the down slow line. Under the bridge can just be made out the bracket signals that carried No. 4's up home signals, as well as No. 2's distant arms. Bewsey Lane is in the background.

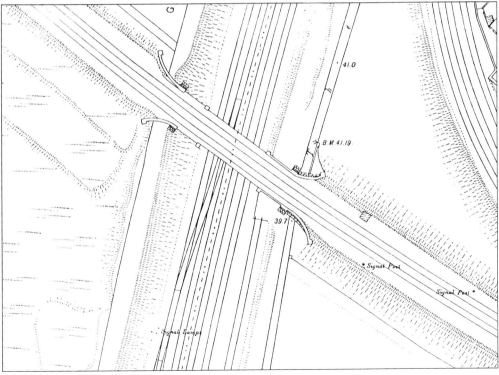

CLC/LNWR BRIDGE, 1888.

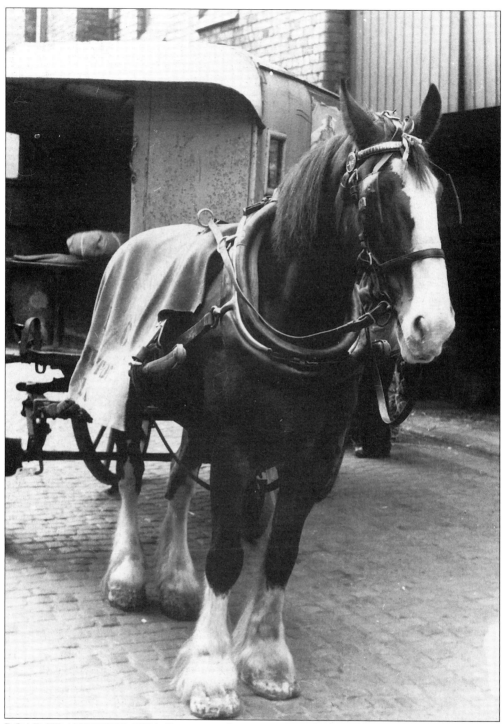

ROAD TRANSPORT, 1954. Pausing at the entrance to the Royal Theatre, is Monty on his rounds. Three years later, aged twenty, this chestnut gelding retired to the RSPCA home at Halewood. In this car-dominated society, it is hard to appreciate that horse and cart were once the chief method of conveyance from goods yards.

CROSFIELD'S WAGONS. In the pre-TV and advert-dominated newspapers, firms advertised wherever they could, hence the vast array of private owners' wagons. The Bank Quay Soap Works, that later became Crosfields, was to the east of the main line and was accessed from both of the LNWR's lines. As business expanded they had their own fleet of small, 0-4-0, tanks engines; one was actually called *Perfection*. The business expanded across the loop in the River Mersey and, from 1916, communicated with it by means of a transporter bridge. It was taken out of use around 1970, and was a listed building. The open wagon was one of twenty ordered in 1908 and was painted in London Red. The white letters had black shading. The tank wagon had vacuum fittings to allow high speed travel in fitted freight trains. With everything going by road these days, Levers have no need of rail tanks or open wagons for transporting the numerous chemicals that are used in their products.

DALLUM LANE STATION, 1950. This view is looking north up Dallam Lane at the side of the Three Pigeons public house, believed to be the booking office of the original station. There is an extensive coal yard to the right and the route of the original line was between the fence and the building. The accompanying 1888 map (opposite) shows how the line crossed Tanner's Lane, Dallam Lane and then went into the coal yard. Much of the movement in the yard would have been done by horses. The brick two storey building at the 'town' end of the yard had evidence of an arched doorway and an inlet for wagons. Some authorities believe that it was a passenger station in the late 1830s. The area is now occupied by a community centre.

DALLAM LANE, 1888.

LEAVING WARRINGTON, 1964. Going tender first south along the up main line on 19 September is Austerity 2-8-0 No. 90390 under Folly Lane Bridge with an express freight. Dallam Branch Sidings signal box is just visible under the bridge. Conceived in the conditions of the last war, these engines were literally 'free of frills', easy to maintain due to the high running plate and constructed under conditions that wouldn't be normally acceptable to unions in peace time. This engine was allocated War Dept. No. 78597 and eventually got its BR number in April 1951. After spells at Hither Green and Newton Heath, it finished its days at Frodingham, before being withdrawn in September 1965.

DALLAM BRANCH SIGNAL BOX, 1969. This was the junction of the two original branches of the Warrington and Newton line. The southern branch eventually formed an end on connection with the Grand Junction Railway line to give today's main line. By the time of this photograph, the engine shed had closed, which meant that the connections in the foreground had been removed. The LMS style box had ninety levers in its hey-day. A new span of Folly Lane Bridge has been built for to give the necessary clearance for the impending overhead wires of electrification.

DALLAM LOCO SHED. This shed opened in 1887, replacing a servicing point adjacent to Bank Quay Station. This view looking south from the coal stacks, in LNWR days, shows the ten road shed with its northlight pattern roof. The majority of engines would be Cauliflower 0-6-0, 18" express goods, or 0-8-0s. A smattering of coal tanks and 2-4-2T would look after the few passenger trips. The turntable and the coaling stage and water tower were to the west and towards the back of the shed. The practise of putting hoops on freight or slow lines' signals stands out clearly, as do the up main line signals.

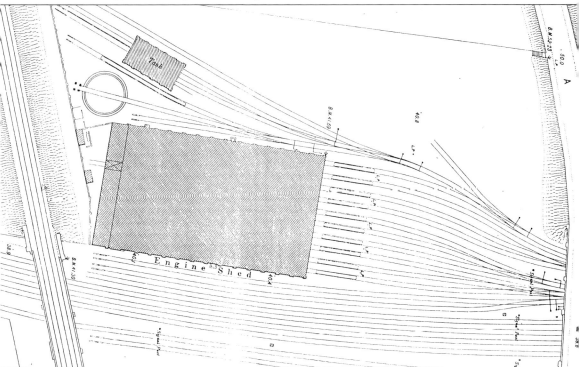

DALLAM LANE LOCO SHED, 1888. Shown when new, this map illustrates the shed as requested by Webb in 1875, capable of holding forty engines at an estimated cost of just over £13,000: the average weekly wage 100 years after opening.

DALLAM SHED, 1967. By the mid 1950s the roof had deteriorated to such an extent that it was replaced in 1957, to be commemorated by a central plaque. The offices were situated at the back of the shed. Moving the turntable freed up some land next to the water tank that was developed into a coaling stage. This was not of the large concrete type but, in later days, consisted of coal stacks on the floor and a conveyer belt that enabled the coal to be loaded into tenders. Some degree of protection against the elements was afforded by a corrugated iron roof.

DALLAM SHED, CODE 8B, 1967. The original shed had a 42 ft turntable but this was later replaced by a larger one (65 ft) which was moved to nearer the front of the shed yard. On it is Stanier 8F 2-8-0 No. 48115, with a sister engine behind it. Heaton Mersey shed was code 9F. Illustrating the mostly freight nature of its allocation, is Standard Class 9F 2-10-0 No. 92055.

DALLAM LANE, 1962. A typical scene on a Sunday morning: full of engines. Those of us occupied in the week perhaps only remember sheds crowded like this. The reality, of course, was that most of the time there were few engines 'on shed' as they were earning their keep, and it was only on Sundays when few trains ran that the sheds were full. Note the creeping encroachment of diesel shunters. The nearby sidings also look full of wagons. The bridge in the background carries the CLC avoiding line for Warrington.

DALLAM'S TURNTABLE, 1967. In readiness for closure the next week or is it the victim of a souvenier hunter? Whatever, Black Five 4-6-0 No. 44672 is minus its shed plate number in August. It was one of the last batch of Black Fives built, at Horwich in February 1950. The foot grips around the perimeter of the well are visible and this was a method of turning locos if the mechanical method being driven by the engine failed.

LNWR No. 18 at DALLAM LANE. In 1882 Webb built an enlarged 17" Coal Engine with outside cylinders and four coupled set of wheels. From 1901 a modification, having two low pressure cylinders inside, was built, later called 'B' class, which had a long overhang ('piano front'). Whale disliked this arrangement and so from 1904 added a pony truck to 26 engines making them 'E' class. Counter weights were added in-between the spokes. No.18, seen here, still has its original buffers, the majority being replaced by the longer Cooke type. This engine was withdrawn in April 1928 but most of the class were converted to 'G' class by the removal of the outside cylinders and an enlarged smoke box.

PASSENGER LOCO AT DALLAM, 1962. Apart from the shuttle to Earlestown and St Helens most passenger duties started, or finished, elsewhere. Ivatt 2-6-2T No. 41213 is seen inside with the smoke vents showing clearly. The electrification warning flashes have already started to appear on the tanks. The apparatus above the cylinders allowed it to be used in 'auto-trains', where the train could be driven by the foot plate crew from a special compartment at the front of a coach. An earlier photograph shows this type of train in action.

L&Y ENGINE AT DALLAM LANE, 1936. Six coupled engines were the mainstay of all railway companies late last century. They were only relegated by the larger 0-8-0s, but, because of their versatility, some of the smaller engines lasted almost to the end of steam. The MR preferred to double head heavy trains and so didn't develop eight coupled locos. A representative of Aspinall's Class 27, introduced in 1889, was No. 12366.

DALLAM LANE, INTERIOR, 1962. Parked right at the end of the shed is Patriot Class 4-6-0 No. 45546 *Fleetwood*, in January. On the next line is 0-6-0T No. 47406. The roof is remarkably clean, letting in plenty of light. The modes of transport of the staff are interesting: a motorbike and side car, several bikes and the shed master's Renault Dauphine, which looks very shiny.

A STUDY IN TANKS. To haul stopping trains, railway companies developed engines with quite large driving wheels so that a good turn of speed could quickly be reached. They had to be small and light to ensure that they could be used on branch lines with weight restrictions. Tank engines were best, as they were built to run in either direction. It is interesting that the designs of two large companies paralleled each other. The LNWR's representative in 1936 was No. 6688, a Webb engine, while that from the L&Y was by Aspinall, Radial Tank, designed No. 50705.

Three
Winwick and the North

Intrepid travellers in the early days of railway had to endure two reversals in passing north from Warrington. Small curves, creating triangles, reduced this to one from 1837 and then completely ten years later.

WINWICK QUAY, 1940. Racing north past a train on the down slow is one of the celebrated Caledonian Blue Coronation Class Pacifics. The question of whether the streamlining kept the smoke out of the driver's view appears to be in doubt. The streamlining casing was 'added on' to the locos' body: on the A4s of the LNER, it was an integral part of the design. In engineering terms, the A4s were considered to offer more air resistance at speeds above 75 mph. In 1937 the first five of the class were introduced, in 1944 the repainting was in an austere black. Smoke deflectors were fitted when streamlining was removed in 1946, repainting in blue and then green followed. Withdrawal occurred in 1963 with something like 1.4 million miles on the clock.

WINWICK QUAY, 1964, illustrating why this was a popular site with railway enthusiasts. On the up slow line and signalled to pass to the sidings, is Fowler 0-6-0 4F No. 44386. A train is also due on the up fast line. On the down side, Austerity 2-8-0 No. 90390 is waiting on the slow line for Class Five 4-6-0 No. 45156 to pass on the fast line. The goods train would then proceed north and, at Winwick Junction, cross onto the same track to Golbourne Junction that the passenger train had taken.

WINWICK QUAY, 1964. Hurrying past on the down main line is Austerity 8F 2-8-0 No. 90509 on 14 July. The small chimney on these engines was deliberate. Riddles, the designer, wanted that to be the deflective talking point rather than other parts of the engine! The broad specification was for a loco capable of hauling 1,000 tons at 40 mph which would have as many fabricated parts as possible and could be assembled with minimal labour. BR bought 730 of this style and painted them black; the number was painted on the cab side.

WINWICK QUAY, 1940. In 1881 the line from Warrington to Winwick Junction was quadrupled and the level crossing at Dallam replaced by a bridge. Some two miles north of Warrington, a set of marshalling sidings was established to the east of the four track main line. The sidings took their name from the adjacent canal repair yard. Ex-LNWR 910 Class No. 6832 is heading north with a train for Earlestown. This 5' 6" class was designed to replace the Samson 2-4-0s on local and branch passenger work; 160 of the tank counterpart of the precursor were built between 1890 and 1897. This one has coal rails fitted, sometime after 1900; originally there was a tool box there. It also has LNWR lamp sockets. In the early days of the Warrington & Newton Railway there were no intermediate stations. After the takeover, the Grand Junction opened one at Winwick. There was a flagpole there which, when the flag was raised, provided the signal for mixed trains to stop. It closed before the end of 1840.

WINWICK QUAY, 1965. An interesting comparison can be made between these 4-6-0 engines. In front is LMS Black Five No. 45436 which was one of the Armstrong Whitworth batch of 1937, costing £6,080 and lasting three more years. BR Class Five No. 73131, in the rear, was built in Derby in 1956 for £28,075; it lasted three months less than the engine it was to replace. The tender carried two tons less coal but 725 more gallons of water. It was fitted with the Caprotti valve gear and poppet valves. BR Standard engines were based upon best practise from all regions. They had simplicity, visibility and accessibility of parts and good axle boxes as paramount. This maximised availability. The tender class engines all had high running plate supported by the boiler, not the main frames.

While the normal Walschaerts valve gear was a reciprocating return, the Caprotti gear was not, being, chiefly, a system of gears to operate the flow of steam to the cylinders. The reduction of wear and tear was an advantage, but a minor irritation was that a differnet system for lubication had to be developed. This was from the right hand rear driving wheel, unfortunately not visible in this view. By the time the Black Five was ordered it was in the second batch of locos from the Tyneside builders and a major redesign of the boiler had taken place. This resulted in the sloping throat plate boiler and a twenty-four element superheater. Most noticable, externally, was the seperation of the top feed and dome. As these modifications resulted in a greater heat surface, they became, with minor modifications, the norm. One disadvantage was the incompatability of the sloping with the virtical throat plates on the first 225 locos. Even though 906 boilers were made for the 842 locos, due to varieties, keeping up with repairs and replacements must have been a logistical problem.

WINWICK QUAY, 1966. On 20 August 1966, ex-LMS Stanier Class Five 4-6-0 No. 44682 hauled the 14.50 from Blackpool North to Stoke-on-Trent past the sidings. When it was built at Horwich in 1950, it was one of the last batch of forty to enter service. Costing £14,175 each, their life span, until November 1967, was remarkably short. While the top half of the signal box is standard LNWR style, the base is wooden. The traditional brick was often dispensed with in areas where ground movements would mean replacement later.

WINWICK QUAY, 1964. Hurrying along the up main line is a representative of Stanier's first design, a year after he was appointed CME for the LMS in 1932. This small (40) class of 2-6-0 engines was a response to the demand for more mixed traffic engines, similar to the large class of successful engines designed by Hughes-Fowler. This example, No. 42959, is fitted with a Fowler tender as used on the Crabs which, as can be seen, was too small for the cab.

WINWICK QUAY, 1962. Restarting, and being directed along the up slow line, is a freight bound for Mold Junction. Jubilee Class 4-6-0 No. 45714 *Revenge* will have brought the train from Patricroft to Earlestown and then down onto the WCML. The sidings here were used for detaching wagons bound for some of Warrington's industries, which would be collected together, and then worked south.

WINWICK JUNCTION, LATER DAYS OF LNWR. A similar scene looking north from the footbridge some years earlier. In charge of its six wheel coaches is Claughton Class 4-6-0 No. 2427 *Duke of Connaught*. These four cylinder engines were built from 1913-1921 at Crewe. They were designed by Bowden-Cooke to haul the heavy trains, especially north of Crewe.

WINWICK JUNCTION, LATE 1950s. Viewed from the over bridge is an up express hauled by Royal Scot Class 4-6-0 No. 46168 *The Girl Guide*. When the line first opened in the 1830s this junction wasn't there. The line joined the Liverpool to Manchester line at, what we today call, Earlestown. Some distance east, at Parkside, a curve north to Wigan meant that trains from London to the North had to negotiate both of these junctions and pass along the L&M. After the construction of the easterly curve at Newton Junction in 1837, only one reversal was necessary, but it wouldn't be until 1847 that the west curve at Parkside eliminated this. To overcome these manoeuvres, a short, two mile cut was made by the LNWR on 1 August 1864, creating junctions at Winwick and Golbourne. Note the writing on the distant factory.

WINWICK JUNCTION, 1940. Racing north is LNWR Pacific 4-6-2 No. 6236 *City of Bradford*, less than a year old with its crimson streamlined cover having gold bands which extended onto the tender. A ton of coal capacity was sacrificed to make them more streamlined, as well as restricting their water capacity to 4,000 gallons; as there were eleven sets of water troughs on the principal Anglo-Scottish line this was not a problem. The casing was removed in December 1947, the loco lasting until March 1964, after covering over one and a half million miles. Of interest is the extensive use of the alloy nickel-steel. Its properties enabled a very large increase in heating surface to be attained with a minimal weight increase. The construction of the boiler from this alloy allowed over two tons to be saved.

WINWICK JUNCTION, 1940. The experimental run of 6201 *Princess Elizabeth* on 16/17 November 1936 between London and Glasgow is now part of railway folklore. It showed that six hour schedules were possible: the addition of an extra thirty minutes was added when the services were accelerated the next year. *City of Bradford* was one of the second batch of engines built after a re-design to add a double chimney. The wartime black livery was added in April 1944. The designer, William Stanier, was indifferent to the streamlining of locos but agreed in order to satisfy the publicity department that was nervous about the attention the LNER expresses were receiving. At that time the LMS was running more stop-start trains, averaging at least 60 mph or more, than the rest of the system put together.

WINWICK JUNCTION AND SIGNAL BOX DIAGRAM. Not only did this forty-five lever frame box control the joining of the Earlestown and the 1864 Golbourne lines, but it also segregated the traffic into fast and slow lines. This view was taken from a train on the down fast line on its way to Wigan. Vulcan Foundry is in the rear. On 28 September 1934, a local train on its way to Vulcan was rammed in the rear by the 17.20 Euston to Blackpool, killing eleven people. The crew of the local train had observed Rule 55 and had just arrived at the box to remind the signal man of their presence when the collision occurred. The resulting inspector's report recommended that track circuiting be installed so that track occupancy was visually displayed in the signal box and trains couldn't therefore be 'forgotten'.

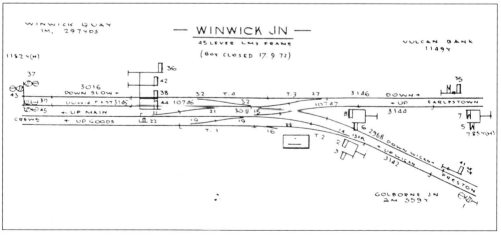

WINWICK JUNCTION, 1959. Standard Class 9F 2-10-0 No. 92015 will have started this coal train from Bold Colliery, on the L&M main line, near St Helens Junction. It will have gone east and at Earlestown, turned south down Vulcan bank. At Winwick Junction it will go onto the up fast and, as seen here, have to be switched onto the up slow to allow faster moving trains to overtake it. The fenced off area in the foreground used to have a siding that a banker, for the one mile long 1 in 85 gradient climb up Vulcan Bank, used to wait in.

WINWICK JUNCTION, 1960. An early autumn train to Llandudno coasts from the Earlestown branch onto the main line. The journey would take a Manchester resident close to three hours, calling at many other North Wales seaside towns on the way. Jubilee 2 Class No. 45699 *Galatea* is sporting a stopping train headcode: unusual for this train.

WINWICK JUNCTION, 1959. Engineering works disrupt train services and so alternative lines are invaluable for continuity of service. Here, due to work on the Runcorn Bridge, the 12.20 Euston to Liverpool (*The Red Rose*) is being diverted via Warrington and Earlestown on 30 May. Hauling the train is Royal Scot Class 4-6-0 No. 46124 *London Scottish*.

ROYAL TRAIN, 1961. Working the train from Manchester Victoria to Euston in May are two 4-6-0s. Unnamed Patriot Class No. 45549 is being piloted by Black Five No. 44773. If the royal family had been on board then a head lamp code of four lamps would be used, but the Queen having returned to London by air, only staff of the royal household were being transported. Interestingly, the footbridge has been dismantled.

DOWN ROYAL SCOT, 1958. Coronation Class Pacific No. 46229 *Duchess of Hamilton* is passing with the 10.00 am departure from Euston. Originally built as a red streamliner in 1938, it underwent repainting to black, blue and green. By this time it was red again, the colour which it kept until its demise in 1964, the year before it had its chambered smoke box door replaced by the standard pattern. This loco went to America for the New York World Fair in 1939, the number 6229 was borrowed by 6220 Coronation.

WINWICK JUNCTION, 1958. The London to Glasgow line was a good line on which to test new types of locomotive. Hauling down the Royal Scot on 30 September are locos 10201 and 10202. They were of the same wheel arrangement (1Co-Co1) as their more powerful sister, 10203, developed initially for the Southern Region. While steam locos had over 120 years experience behind them, diesel locos were still in their infancy here and so reliability was a problem.

GOLBORNE JUNCTION, 1962. Seven miles north of Warrington and the Golbourne-Winwick link rejoins the original 1832 Parkside-Wigan line. Sidings on the L&M line allowed slower moving trains to be diverted onto it and to be overtaken by faster trains on the main line. An up fitted freight hauled by Black Five 4-6-0 No. 45072 is taking the Winwick line, with the Lowton line to the right. Belonging to a small group of five engines built at Crewe in 1935 at a cost of £6,150, it gave sterling service until September 1967.

GOLBORNE JUNCTION, 1962. Heading north along the line from Winwick Junction is Hughes-Fowler Crab 2-6-0 No. 42810 with an excursion on 28 July. On the left is the line from Lowton and in front, will be the junction and the division into eastern fast lines and western slow lines.

GOLBORNE, 1962. Looking north towards Golbourne Station, an express passes along the lines that were quadrupled from here to Wigan between 1888 and 1894. The small town boasted LNWR as well as GCR stations. By the time this photograph was taken, on 16 June, both stations had closed. Class 5 4-6-0 No. 45258 would have a free run from Wigan to Warrington. In 1936, Armstrong Whitworth built this engine as one of a batch of 226, lasting until March 1968. The new engine and tender cost £6,050.

GOLBORNE JUNCTION SIGNAL BOX, 1971. Towering some 18 ft above rail level was this forty-eight lever frame box. Its height was necessary due to sighting problems: trains needed to be visually seen. At this junction the fast lines (to Winwick) were crossed by the slow lines (to Lowton). This is a type 4 box with the barge board set directly over the boards and finials inserted into them. The middle panes of glass were fixed and to enable cleaning, a walk way was provided. It survived until 1972.

GOLBORNE SOUTH STATION, 1961. The porter and booking clerk sells the last ticket on 6 February 1961, the purchaser of which may have travelled to Newton-le-Willows. For over one hundred years it was known as 'Golborne', LNWR if necessary, until BR added the suffix in 1949. This distinguished it from the ex-GCR station to the north which had closed nine years earlier, on 3 March.

Four
West of Sankey Viaduct

The history of the world's first regular passenger line worked by locos has often been written about, and there is little that I can add to that. What follows is an account of part of it, from Huyton to Kenyon Junctions. After opening between Crown Street (Liverpool) and Liverpool Road (Manchester) in 1830, it acted as a backbone in those early days for other lines to join onto in the desire to reach Lancashire's chief cities. So, in 1831 the Kenyon and Leigh Joint Railway, followed by the Warrington and Newton Railway, branched from it. This was followed in 1832 by a spur to the St Helens and Runcorn Gap Railway at Sutton and, later, the Wigan Branch Railway from Parkside.

HUYTON STATION IN LNWR DAYS. This was one of the original L&M stopping places when the line opened in 1830. To call it a station in those early days would have been wrong. It consisted of a crossing with the road and there would have been a small dwelling that the passengers could use as a waiting room. Platforms, if they existed, were rudimentary. Proper platforms and station buildings were added some time later, with the line becoming quadrupled in the early 1870s to cope with the anticipated traffic from the nearby branch to St Helens. Some half a mile east of the station is the site of the departure of the LNWR's line north east to St Helens. It opened to passengers at the start of 1872 and to goods trains two weeks earlier.

HUYTON STATION, 1985. This view, looking towards the buildings on the Liverpool platform, the ex-fast lines, shows them shorn of their canopies. The signals are at the end of the Manchester bound platform. The line of the present railway was not that proposed by Lawrence and Stephenson in their 1824 prospectus; that line would have gone further north through Bootle, Fazackerley, Eccleston and Haydock on its way to Salford. The bill was withdrawn chiefly due to the opposition of the interested parties over which area it was to pass. Another bill, a year later, had a route to the south, close to that suggested by William James in 1822. This was successful as it didn't pass through the Croxteth and Knowsley estates nor did it affect the principal waterways in the area: the Duke of Bridgewater's canal, Mersey and Irwell Navigation and the Leeds and Liverpool canal. It actually did not interfere with a single street in Liverpool and was proposed to terminate near New Bailey prison in Salford, not even entering Manchester at all!

HUYTON QUARRY, 1925. A station 'at the bottom of Whiston incline' existed by 1838, which later became Huyton Quarry. Drawing into the Manchester platform is a pre-grouping train. This was the sight of an accident in 1874 when two trains came into contact with each other while passing. It was later discovered that the space between the up and down lines was no more than 4 ft 5 ins, when it should be 6 ft.

HUYTON QUARRY, 1966. In a view looking east are the goods sidings some eight years after the station's closure. Not only was there a quarry to the north, but also mineral workings some distance to the south. During permanent way work in 1976, a crane accidentally demolished the signal box.

HUYTON QUARRY, 1964. Sporting headcode 1M63 (the 10.40 Hull to Liverpool) is the especially Swindon built six car Trans-Pennine DMU. The train consisted of two driving motor units, two trailers, a powered guard and second class coach and a buffet car. The motors produced 1,380 hp and the unit provided 316 seats. In 1951 this service would have arrived at Manchester's Exchange at 2.13 pm and at Lime Street at 3.15 pm. The Leeds to Manchester journey would take 83 minutes: these units reduced it to 68 minutes, with stops at Stalybridge and Huddersfield. It wasn't until the re-modelling of junctions in Yorkshire that the elusive hour schedule was achieved in the late 1980s. When these units were first introduced in 1961 there was an increase in patronage of 45 per cent from Leeds. So successful is this route in the mid 1990s that it is to be electrified.

KENDRICK CROSS GATE, LATER RAINHILL. One reason why there was a station at Rainhill, as it became known as from 1844, if not earlier, was because of the crossing of the line by the turnpike road to Warrington. As neither could be diverted to allow a right angled crossing, the bridge was built 'on the skew' – possibly the first of its kind over a main line railway. Wayside stations only came to be known by 'official' names when timetables and tickets were printed and later, buildings were developed for passengers' comfort. In fact, in those early days, 'The man merely has to open and shut the gate, the train stops, takes up passengers, and goes on'. This was the evidence that the L&M's Henry Booth gave to the select committee on railway operations. He was explaining why no real record of departure times from intermediate stations was kept.

RAINHILL STATION, LATE 1880s, LOOKING EAST. The trials are another reason why this place is famous. To settle the argument between fixed engines pulling the train along with a rope and locomotives, a prize of £500 was offered. From 6 October 1829, the trials took place on a piece of level track less than two miles long. Each locomotive had to haul three times its own weight, at not less than 10 mph, over the distance of Liverpool to Manchester, and return; about forty trips of the course were needed. Shown looking east from the Skew Bridge are the main buildings on the platform that most people travelling on to Liverpool would be expected to use. There is a fine example of a lattice footbridge for passengers; note also the tall signal post to aid visibility over the bridge.

PRIVATE-OWNER WAGONS. This coal wagon was built by the Gloucester Carriage and Wagon Works in February 1923. Oddly, it still carried the pre-grouping name. The main journeys were to Garston and Canada Docks and back again when empty. It was painted mostly grey, with black iron work and white letters shaded with black.

RAINHILL STATION, 1936. Looking towards Liverpool is an ex-LNWR G Class engine passing the gas works. The photograph was taken from the footbridge at the eastern end of the station. While the trials resolved the difficulty between fixed and moving engines, it was still thought that up gradients that fixed engines would be necessary. However, during the event, the winner, *Rocket*, went up the 1 in 96 Whiston inclined plane several times.

RAINHILL STATION, 1958. Seen from the western footbridge in March is Jubilee Class 4-6-0 No. 45708 *Resolution*, possibly on a Leeds to Liverpool train. This Crewe built engine lasted from June 1936 until February 1964. The station buildings are instantly recognisable: little has changed today.

RAINHILL STATION, 1957. At just after 5.20 pm on 5 April, Stanier 2 cylinder 2-6-4T No. 42602 leaves with the 4.50 pm Lime Street all stations to Earlestown, arriving at 5.37 pm. A few miles back down the line it would have been passed on the fast line by the 5.00 pm from Liverpool to Newcastle. That too called at Earlestown, at 5.20pm.

NEAR RAINHILL, SUNDAY 11 AUGUST 1968. Over thirty years old and on its way to near its 'birth place', Vulcan Foundry, is Black Five 4-6-0 No. 45110 with an enthusiast's special from Lime Street, Liverpool to Carlisle to mark the end of steam on BR. The builders constructed two batches of fifty Universal (go anywhere, do anything) locos in 1934/5 and 1935/6. When ordered at the price of £6,150, including tender, they were given the classification 5P5F as they could run over 70 per cent of LMS lines.

RAINHILL SIGNAL BOX. This is a standard LNWR type 4 box with a timber cabin on top of a brick base, opened in 1896, with twenty-five levers. The box controlled the line between Whiston station in the west, which closed in 1961, and Lea Green in the east. Originally this opened as Top of Sutton Inclined Plane before changing its name first to Lea Green, then Sutton in 1844 and finally, Lea Green in 1848. The station closed on 7 March 1965. The box is still in use today.

Table **128**

ST. HELENS (Shaw Street) TO ST. HELENS JUNCTION
Weekdays only.   Third Class Only (except where otherwise shown).

Miles		**A**					**SX**	**SO SO SX SO**				**SX SX**	**B**	**SO**
		a.m. a.m. a.m. a.m. a.m. a.m.						a.m. noon p.m. p.m.	p.m. p.m. p.m. p.m.			p.m. p.m. p.m. p.m.	p.m.	p.m.
0	St. Helens Shaw St. ......dep.	5 15 6 40 7 19 8 0 9 0 10 55	.	10 55 12 0 1 0 1 5	2 10 3 40 5 26 5 40 6 20 6 50 8 58 10 45	.	11 8
¾	Peasley Cross	... ... 10 57		10 57 ... 1 2 1 7	2 12 ... 5 28 5 42 6 24	.	...
1¼	Sutton Oak	... 6 43 7 22 ... 9 3 10 59	...	10 59 12 3 1 4 1 9	2 14 ... 5 30 5 44 6 26 6 53	.	...
2	St. Helens Junction ....arr.	5 22 6 47 7 26 8 6 9 7 11 3	...	11 3 12 7 1 8 1 13	2 18 3 47 5 34 5 48 6 30 6 57 9 6 10 52	...	11 15
10	125 Warrington (Bank Quay) arr.	5 43 7 17 . 8 46 9 27 11 33	.	11 27 12 33 1 34 1 41	3X20 4F55 5 54 6 33 7 19 8 4 9 27 11 15	.	...
22	125 Manchester (Exchange) ,,	7 21 7 45 8 32 8 52 9 49 11 43	...	11 43 12 54 2 8 2 15	2 57 4 39 6J43 ... 7 36 7 50 10T0 ...	...	...
13	125 Liverpool (Lime Street) ,,	6 50 . 8 3 9 15 9 45 12 32	.	. 12 39 2 9 2 9	3 48 5F 06S030 6 30 7 15 8 18 10 36 11SX52	...	11 58

A—Conveys First and Third Class passengers.
B—On Saturdays conveys First and Third Class passengers.
D—On September 22nd departs Warrington 11.5 a.m.
F—On Saturdays arrives Warrington 5.48 p.m., Liverpool (Lime Street) 5.27 p.m.
J—On Saturdays arrives Manchester (Exchange) 6.35 p.m.
X—On Saturdays arrives Warrington 3.25 p.m.

For other trains between St. Helens Shaw Street and Sutton Oak see Table 136.

Table **128**—*continued*

ST. HELENS JUNCTION TO ST. HELENS (Shaw Street)
Weekdays only.   Third Class Only (except where otherwise shown)

Miles		**SO SX SO**					**B** **SX SX**			**SO**		
		a.m. a.m. a.m. a.m. a.m. a.m.	p.m. p.m. p.m. p.m. p.m.	p.m. p.m. p.m. p.m. p.m.	p.m.		
—	125 Liverpool (Lime Street) dep.	5 50 7 20 7 45 . 10S00	12 10 1 0 1 30 .	3 50 4 50 . 5 35 6 55 8 35 .	10 45 .	...	...
—	125 Manchester (Exchange) ,,	6 5 7 10 ... 9 0 10 25 11 45	12 50 12 53 2 29 3SX20	4 R5 5 0 5 15 5 43 7 1 9 2 9 10 10 40 ...	...	...
—	125 Warrington (Bank Quay) ,,	7 20 7 50 8 15 9 5 10 45 12 00	1 5 1 5 2 18 3 24 4 25	5 23 5 27 6 10 6S039 9 20 10 16 ...	...	...
0	St. Helens Junction ....dep.	7 44 8 9 8 40 9 40 11 7 12 25	1 27 1 35 3 10 4 22	4 46 5 43 6 0 6 45 7 43 9 43 10 36 11 33	...	...	...
¾	Sutton Oak	7 46 8 11 8 42 9 42 11 9 12 27	1 29 1 37 . 4 24	4 48 5 46 6 2 6 47 7 45 .	.	...	...
1¼	Peasley Cross	7 48 8 13 ... 9 44 ...	1 31 1 39 ... 4 26	4 50 ... 6 4 ... 7 47 ...	...	...	...
2	St. Helens Shaw St. ....arr.	7 52 8 17 8 47 9 48 11 14 12 32	1 35 1 43 3 17 4 30	4 54 5 51 6 8 6 52 7 51 9 52 10 45 11 41	.	...	.

R—On Saturdays departs Manchester (Exchange) 3.48 p.m.
SO—Saturdays only.   **SX**—Saturdays excepted.
T—On Saturdays arrives Manchester (Ex.) 10.4 p.m.

TIMETABLE, 1951. Showing the 'Junction Bus'.

ST HELENS JUNCTION. Originally opened as Bottom of Sutton Incline, its name changed sometime around 1832/33. The Runcorn Gap to St Helens line passed over the line on a fancy bridge, with a simple spur allowing north to east movements. The overhead line was doubled in 1849 and the new intersection bridge probably dates from then as well. In 1881/2 the spur connecting the two lines was altered so that trains from the main line passed under the branch before coming up to meet it: this increased the capacity of the junction by removing a crossing. The spur lasted until 2 March 1969. This picture is of Webb 2-2-2-0 engine on the L&M line with some empty stock and a DX Class 0-6-0 engine at the head of a coal train on the Widnes-St Helens line; the people are waiting to see the royal train go by, sometime in the 1880s or 1890s. The signals for the Widnes line indicate that it is quadruple at that point.

ST HELENS JUNCTION, 1953. Looking west from the platform's end is Box No.1 and the up home signals, with a tall repeater arm to aid visibility. The large (sixty four levers) typical LNWR box controlled a section of the main line and the joining of the quadruple lines from the north. Warrington's power box took over its functions in 1972. In the middle of a motor train (the 'Junction Bus') is Stanier 2-6-2T No. 41321. It will have left St Helens a short while ago and is about to pass onto the up main line. After a short trip along the main line it will probably pass south at Earlestown towards Warrington. There was a short bay that some of the two coach trains used, accessed from the points that the bogie of the leading coach is passing over. The driver was in the compartment at the front of the leading coach.

COLLINS GREEN, *c*. 1950. This was one of the original stations that was shown in the February 1831 timetable, which was closed after 120 years on 2 April 1951. Typical LNWR wooden buildings and a fine lattice footbridge are shown in a view looking towards Manchester. There was a small signal cabin at the end of the Liverpool platform. Apart from making a block post on the main line, the box also controlled the branch to Collins Green colliery. Its closure in the mid 1960s led to the box's demise.

ST HELENS JUNCTION, 1951. Looking east is the Liverpool platform. There were bays at the end of both platforms and the buildings on the left and the footbridge are still in use. Authorised but never built, were links to the line going south to Widnes and sidings to facilitate exchange of traffic. The latter were developed for new sheds and workshops.

SANKEY VIADUCT, 1911. Due to the geology of the valley, around 200 piles were driven down to a depth of between 20-30 feet. The piers are splayed below the string line, beneath which is another string course. Pilaster strips divide the spandrel walls and the cornice is corbelled. The arches are built on sandstone slabs and are brick faced with stone. The whole viaduct cost £45,000. This photograph shows the true proportions of the viaduct, rather than the more romantic drawing. The rail-connected Sankey Sugar Works is visible through the arches, the factory probably occupying the former site of Muspratt's Vitriol Works: the name lives on with the houses in nearby Vitriol Square!

The two modes of transport shown determined the face of South Lancashire. The Sankey Brook Navigation opened in 1757 and was a very profitable enterprise. It would be another seventy years before its supremacy was challenged by the Liverpool to Manchester line and its branches. The day is 11 August 1968 and the train marks the end of an era: it is the last steam hauled train. The engine was built thirty-three years ago at nearby Vulcan Foundry.

SANKEY VIADUCT. The foundations of this viaduct were laid in 1828 as the line had to cross a valley and the Sankey Brook. This contained the 1757 canal from collieries in the St Helens area to the River Mersey, firstly near Warrington, then at Fidler's Ferry and finally at Runcorn Gap, Widnes. The viaduct is approached from the east on a 900 ft long embankment which leads to the nine, 50 ft arches taking the line some 50 ft above the canal, which was diverted to pass through the third.

SANKEY VIADUCT, 1960. Early drawings in the monthly supplement of *The Penny Magazine of the Society for the Diffusion of Useful Knowledge*, show a small wooden viaduct to the west of the stone one: presumably this was filled in soon after opening. On the extreme right is the site of the original Viaduct Foundry; this was to form part of the wagon works after the LNWR leased it from 1853. On the viaduct is Jinty 0-6-0T No. 47298 shunting the wagon works.

Five
Earlestown and Vulcan

EARLESTOWN, 1960. This curve is one of the world's oldest passenger railway junctions, dating from June 1831. During 1960/61, Runcorn Bridge was refurbished and made ready for electrification. Then the clock was turned back almost 100 years to the 1860s, before it was built. At that time, London bound trains passed around this tight curve, via Warrington to Crewe. Following a similar path with a relief Red Rose, is Princess Class No. 46203 *Princess Margaret Rose*. These engines were built by the LMS to cope with the rigours of heavy trains to Scotland. Until then the Fowler built Royal Scot Class had to be changed at Carlisle. The larger grate and wide fire box demanded a trailing pony truck, resulting in the pacific wheel arrangement: this one was built at Crewe in 1935, which can now be seen in crimson lake at the Midland Railway Centre at Buttersley.

VIADUCT STATION. This was the name in the 1831 timetable and it wouldn't be until December 1861 that the current name of Earlestown appeared. Names in those intervening years were Warrington Junction and Newton Junction. Confusion was caused due to the arrival, from the south, of the Newton & Warrington Railway on 25 July 1831. This turn of the century view is east along the L&M main line towards Manchester. On the right is the Liverpool curve to Warrington.

EARLESTOWN STATION, 1972, seen from the Manchester platform, looking towards Liverpool. To the right is Railway Street, behind the rather rudimentary facilities, now replaced by a bus stop shelter. The booking office used to be in the ornate buildings on the island platform, now it is just outside the station's entrance. From there a footbridge enabled the three other platforms at the junction to be accessed. Passengers have to go along a footpath across a quarter of a mile to reach the Manchester curve platforms. Tall semaphore signals are necessary due to sighting problems caused by the footbridge.

EARLESTOWN, 1960. Rebuilt Patriot 4-6-0 No. 45535 *Sir Herbert Walker KCB* restarts a Newcastle to Liverpool train. Until the station was reconstructed, the furthest away of the 1847 built cottages was the booking office. The tall LNWR signals, with their smaller, lower repeater arms, show up well.

EARLESTOWN, 1960. The foot plate crew of Jubilee No. 45663 *Jervis* look at the shape of things to come. The twenty-five year old Crewe built engine is on a Newcastle to Liverpool train. Seen here on crew training, from the start of January the next year, the Trans-Pennine units will take over the Hull to Liverpool service. The five trains each way from Hull, and five more starting from Leeds, led to a 45 per cent increase in passengers from the Yorkshire towns.

EARLESTOWN, LIVERPOOL CURVE, 1955. This was taken from a passing Manchester to Liverpool train. There are two trains, both apparently wanting to go the same way, in the Liverpool curve platforms. On the right is a 2-6-4T, waiting for the photographer's train to proceed. It will then join the main line and will probably stop at all stations to Liverpool Lime Street. The left hand train looks to be a smaller tank, a 2-6-2T, on the St Helens to Warrington service.

EARLESTOWN, 1930. Prior to the arrival of Stanier at the LMS, motor trains were handled by locos like this Webb 5' 6" 2-4-2T or 910' class built from 1890. Coal rails have been fitted. These were push-pull fitted to allow ease of working at the ends of the journeys. Still in existence are the Gothic style Yorkshire stone station facilities buildings which used to contain the booking office and waiting room. They were rumoured to have been the LNWR's board room and, before that, a chapel or a school. This platform and the footbridge have been demolished.

EARLESTOWN, PLATFORM 5, 1965. On 4 July 1837, the Grand Junction Railway opened this south to east curve. This allowed trains from Manchester to get to Birmingham and, ultimately, London. It is a very tight curve as the check rails indicate. This pair of platforms was some distance from the main buildings. Not only were passengers faced with a long walk but they had to cross over the Haydock Branch and then over another footbridge to get to the Warrington platform. So large was the land in the triangle that it contained several houses at one stage; there are several allotments in it now. Arriving from Warrington is Jubilee Class No. 45652 *Hawke* on its way to Wigan North Western.

EARLESTOWN, MANCHESTER CURVE, 1966. Standard Class 5 4-6-0 No. 73144 is waiting to take the 11.30 from Llandudno to Manchester. This curve was altered in 1972/3 by the demolition of the station buildings to make way for the supporting masts of the overhead wire electrification.

LNWR CLUB CAR. This particular coach at Abergele was an ex-American special, first from the prestigious trains the company ran from London to Liverpool Riverside to connect with the trans-Atlantic steamers around the turn of the century. It was made into a Club Car for the North Wales trains from Llandudno to Manchester. These passed from Exchange, along the L&M to Earlestown and then went via Warrington to Chester and North Wales. In 1910 the two hour, eighty mile outward journey for a business man would start from Llandudno at 8.10 am with a similar return journey at 4.55 pm.

HAYDOCK COLLIERY LINE, 1964. An unidentified 4F and brake van cross the ungated Wargrave Road and take the north to east curve from the Haydock Branch. Viewed from the roof of the local cinema, now a snooker hall, are parts of Earlestown station. In the middle distance is the footbridge over the Manchester Curve with its 1902 buildings at some distance from the main station. In the bottom right is the flat crossing, guarded by the tall signal.

HAYDOCK CROSSING, 1964. A very grimy and unidentifiable Austerity 0-6-0ST belonging to the National Coal Board crosses the L&M main line at the eastern end of Earlestown station. This branch opened in May 1831; the L&M board ruled against a crossing on the level. The branch connected with the main line in the Manchester direction and, from 1832, directly onto the W&N across the L&M on the flat. After accidents there a bridge was suggested. The solution, from July 1838, was to erect a tall flagpole and for the policeman to hoist a distinctly coloured flag whenever a coal train was crossing.

HAYDOCK COLLIERY BRANCH, 1960. The NCB's 0-6-0ST *King*, brings a train load of coal destined for Sankey Sugar Works down from Haydock Colliery. The outer home signal was controlled by Earlestown's No. 3 box and it guarded the entrance to the main line. The homes on the left are in King Street.

HAYDOCK BRANCH, 1969. This view is along the backs of homes in King Street towards Bridge Street, with the Manchester platform on the left. So important was this line that it was double through the streets of Earlestown, as the gaps in the bridge illustrate. A landscaped car park now occupies the land behind the houses. (Photograph by courtesy of Neil Frazer)

EARLESTOWN NO. 3 BOX, HAYDOCK COLLIERY CROSSING, 1967. Looking not much different than a garden shed is box No. 3, whose twelve levers controlled the flat crossing by a system of signals and trap points. This was the official rail route to the Newton Racecourse Station until it closed in 1898, nine years after Haydock Park opened. The buildings were the official homes for the signalman. This is now the station car park.

TROUBLE AT THE CROSSING, 1959. Perhaps the horse drawn tramway that was in operation before the railway meant that the colliery was always going to cross the main line on the flat, however unsafe it was. On 29 December the trap points to protect the main line proved their worth. Engine No. 43615, from Dallam, was unable to brake its load of forty full coal wagons. They overpowered it, derailed the tender first and then the wagons piled into the station master's back garden across Wargrave Road, overturning the engine in the process. It took several days to get things right again.

EARLESTOWN'S SIGNAL BOXES

The following four boxes are straight out of the LNWR book: wood cabin on a brick base. The company had production down to a fine art, even to the extent of making their own bricks. They all had company tappet frames with different numbers of levers in them. As they have free barge boards, sliding windows and no walkways, they date from the 1902 station rebuild and are designated type 5. Warrington's power box took over their functions from 1972.

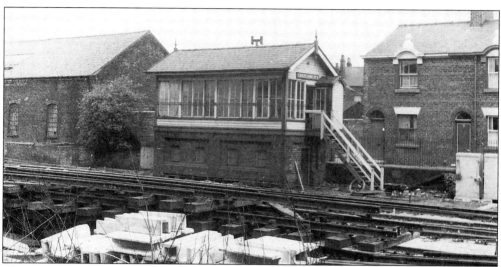

EARLESTOWN NO. 4 BOX, LIVERPOOL JUNCTION. This is slightly over a quarter of a mile east of No. 5 box, adjacent to the up platform. Its forty levers controlled the Liverpool Junction on the main line, the access to the carriage works, and the start of the down goods loops and sidings. The homes to the rear are in Chemical Street.

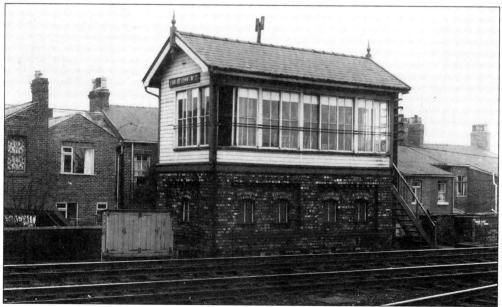

EARLESTOWN NO. 2 BOX, MANCHESTER JUNCTION. This thirty-five lever box was situated just beyond the Manchester end of the up platform, where the 1837 curve from the Warrington & Newton line met the Liverpool & Manchester.

EARLESTOWN NO. 1 BOX, WARRINGTON JUNCTION, situated south of the station where the Manchester and Liverpool lines separate. In between them is the largest box, with fifty-two levers, with the most to do. Its main job was to control the curves, the start of the western goods loop, and the connection across the Liverpool curve to Haydock Colliery to the north. The white diamond on the post with the BR signal means that it is track circuited and a train's presence there will be shown up on an illuminated panel in the box.

EARLESTOWN NO. 5 BOX. This is to the west of the station. At almost a mile east of Collins Green it controls the extensive sidings and lines to private firms like the Sankey Sugar Co., as well as the joining of the down goods loops and sidings to the main line. With thirty-three levers it was the smallest of the group.

EARLESTOWN WAGON WORKS. A foundry, accessed from Pepper Alley Lane, had been established to the east of the Sankey Viaduct soon after the L&M opened. The firm of Jones, Turner and Evans made pumps for local mines and a number of locomotives. Early in the 1850s the LNWR decided to look at the works due to the inadequacies of Crewe. As a consequence, the Viaduct Foundry site was leased, and later bought, and the Newton Wagon Works established. Staff were transferred from the Ordsall Lane site, residential accommodation nearby expanded and the township of Earlestown began to take shape. At the turn of the century approximately 2,000 people worked there. Four thousand new wagons were made annually as well as 13,000 heavy repairs and 200-300 new horse drawn vehicles. As can be imagined, the site and the size of the buildings substantially increased: 100 years after opening the original eight acres had grown to thirty-six. For efficiency, semi-production line methods of construction were employed: as the picture shows, piles of wood were cut to size and drilled for ease of building.

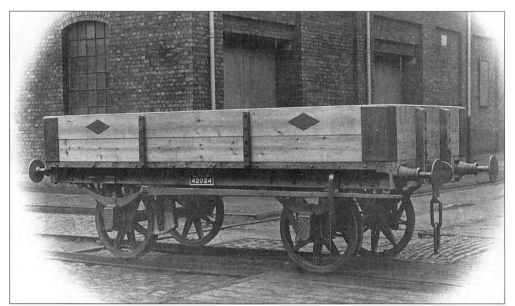

EARLESTOWN PRODUCT. Name changes occurred when the original lane became Earle Street and the station became Earlestown. These reflected not only the growth of the area for workers, but also the LNWR director they were complimenting. After the grouping, the works became the principal LMSR factory for heavy repairs and for the manufacture of door-to-door containers. This two plank wagon was built there in 100 minutes.

EARLESTOWN'S MANAGEMENT, 1953. This view was taken at the wooden Warnford Hall building in the recreation ground across Earle Street from the works. At one corner is the Griffin pub, built and owned by the LNWR. Now the works is the Deacon Trading estate and the 'rec' is a local cricket club. It, like other railway companies, was paternalistic towards its employees, providing hospitals and recreational facilities.

EARLESTOWN WAGON WORKS, 1961. This small building was to house the works' shunter, seen at work on the viaduct. Waiting to take the daily test train is Standard Mogul No. 76079. It was pouring with rain when the picture was taken.

EARLESTOWN TEST TRAIN, 1961. Every day a train ran to Lostock Hall Junction and back. It conveyed the previous day's newly repaired wagons from the Viaduct works. Also in the train were works staff who kept a sharp lookout for hot axle boxes and carried out minor repairs or adjustments on any of the numerous goods loops en route. Sutton Oak's Standard Class 4 No. 76023 is in charge.

EARLESTOWN, WARRINGTON JUNCTION, 1965. Train 1Z42 from Watford to Aintree, for the Grand National, is taking the Liverpool curve at the junction. Hauling the train is BR Standard Class 4-6-2 No. 70052 *Firth of Tay*. It would pass along the L&M to Olive Mount Junction and then turn north to join the Bootle Branch. At Southport Junction in Bootle it will pass onto the ex-L&Y line only to leave it at Seaforth and pass along the North Mersey line to Sefton Junction. Finally, it would go down to the ex-L&Y line from Liverpool to Preston to arrive at Aintree, Sefton Arms Station.

VULCAN HALT. Passing down the 1 in 85 Vulcan Bank with a mixed freight in the mid 1960s, is Jubilee Class 4-6-0 No. 45562 *Alberta*. The wooden platforms were opened on 1 November 1912 for the workers at the adjacent foundry, closing on 14 June 1965. It was here that many famous steam and later, diesel locos were built. Ironically, this engine was built by the North British Loco Co. in 1934, giving good service until November 1967.

VULCAN HALT, 1962. The Warrington to St Helens service was taken over by DMUs in 1961 and a regular pattern established. However, the finishing times at Vulcan Foundry didn't fit in, so two steam push and pull workings were retained. They also performed local pick up freights. Leaving for Warrington in April is Standard Class 2 2-6-2T No. 84000.

VULCAN HALT, 1960. One morning in December, Stanier 2-6-2T No. 41288 derailed its pony truck on the crossover here. This resulted in its LHS steamcocks being jammed open, seen here spraying steam all over the place. Single line working had to be introduced. Jubilee Class 4-6-0 No. 45645 *Collingwood* is easing past, with inches to spare, pulling the 8.35 train from Manchester Exchange to Holyhead.

Six

Parkside and Beyond

The memorial at Parkside is to a fatality on the opening of the Liverpool to Manchester line on 15 September 1830. When the Grand Juction Railway was opened from Birmingham to Warrington in 1837, there was no ceremony whatsoever. It was announced that the directors intended that there should be no public rejoicing on that occasion as they wished to mark their respect for the late Mr Huskisson.

PARKSIDE, 1965. Passing the site of the Huskisson Memorial on 8 June, is Class Five 4-6-0 No. 45285. Its train, the 4.30 'Club Train', was intended for North Wales towns such as Rhyl, Colwyn Bay and Llandudno, but took over two hours to get there. While the junction on the left to Wigan is still in use, the signal box (Parkside No. 1) has been demolished and vegetation obscures the memorial.

NEWTON LE WILLOWS, 1905. From the east, the main line passes over the Newton Road (turnpike road from Wigan to Warrington) and the River Deane on a five arch stone viaduct. The modest two platform station opened as Newton with the line. In 1868 it became Newton Bridge and, twenty years later, it took on its present name. On the Manchester side are the original sandstone station buildings, although by now they are showing some signs of wear. Since this view the facilities on the Liverpool platform have been replaced by a bus stop shelter. There were the typical L&M slated canopies for passengers' protection.

NEWTON LE WILLOWS, c. 1950. Due to the meeting of both the Newton & Warrington Railway in the west, and the Wigan Branch Railway in the east, to the L&M, Newton was effectively placed in between east and west triangles. Up to 1864, London to the north trains passed through here. In fact, until the Manchester-Birmingham line opened in 1843 this was the route south. The construction of the Golbourne-Winwick link in 1864 by the LNWR reduced the bottleneck on the L&M main line by providing a direct line for north to south trains.

NEWTON LE WILLOWS, 1947. Arriving, with what is probably the 11.25 SO from Manchester Exchange is LNWR Coal Tank 0-6-2 No. 7737 on 22 April. This bay platform and a small goods yard were on the up side. With the closure of the former LNWR line through Latchford, and the different pattern in mining, this stretch of line is very busy. These tracks are not only used by Liverpool to Manchester trains, but also coal trains for Fiddler's Ferry power station and the empties. They flit from north to south along this line in a manner reminiscent of former times.

PARKSIDE WEST CURVE, 1961. Someone waking after over 120 years of sleep would not find this picture too puzzling. While this is a diversion from the main line from Blackpool to Euston, in those early days, this would have been the only route. Still with its straight smoke deflectors is Patriot 4-6-0 No. 45520 *Llandudno* in January. Number 2 signal box also controlled the entrance to the adjacent colliery before being taken over by Newton-le-Willows box, which was in turn superseded by Warrington's power box in 1972. The M6 now strides across this view.

NEWTON-LE-WILLOWS, 1992. Class 20s Nos 20.081 and 20.016 leave the about-to-close colliery at Parkside with the last rail shipment on 26 October. They are emerging from the loops to pass west along the L&M line. When BR put forward their modernisation programme in 1955, this class of locomotive was the first main line diesel to be built. Over a ten year period, nearby Vulcan Foundry built 150 out of a total of 228. The rear engine, dating from June 1958, was the oldest main line loco in BR's service. The section from Earlestown, east along the L&M and the Parkside West Curve, are all electrified by OHW to allow it, ironically, to be used for diversions from the Golbourne-Winwick link.

PARKSIDE COLLIERY, 1964. Austerity 2-8-0 No. 90212 leaves the brand new colliery with the first train load of coal shipped from there in March. In the twenty-eight years between these two pictures there have been enormous changes. Deep mining has virtually ceased, steel mineral wagons have given way to hoppers and steam has vanished from the system. The one year old M6, in the background, is practically devoid of traffic.

PARKSIDE STATION, 1830s. This official print shows an engine at the only stopping point at which coke and water were available between Liverpool and Manchester. It shows what passed for a station in those days. This was just east of the junction of the 1832 single track Wigan Branch Railway with the L&M. Then the L&M gave £35 towards the cost of building a waiting room 'on the sunny side of the road' instead of under the rock on the south side.

PARKSIDE, 1956. This easterly view shows the main Liverpool to Manchester line and the branch off to the left to Wigan, controlled by No.1 box. This branch was doubled in 1838 when it was extended to Preston. In 1839 a new station was built jointly between the L&M, GJR and the NUR, a little to the east of the existing one. Until the start of 1847, trains for the west coast main line travelled a short distance over the L&M through Newton and reversed at Parkside. From then, a west to north curve opened to enable Liverpool-Wigan workings. The station closed on 1 May 1878.

LOWTON, (LNWR). This opened as Preston Junction until February 1877, when it became Lowton and Preston Junction. It closed, as many stations did, for the latter part of the First World War (for 25 months from 1 January 1917), re-opening as Lowton (LNWR). It closed on 26 September 1949. Looking north are the tall, but otherwise standard LNWR signal box and signals, made necessary by the adjacent road bridge. The platforms can just be made out beyond the bridge. Signalled is the 1847 west to north, Parkside West Curve to Earlestown. Currently, two early morning passenger trains per day from Wigan to Liverpool use this route, which has OHW. The other route is the 1832 east to north, Wigan Branch Railway. Some two miles to the north east was the station on the ex-GC line from Glazebrook-Wigan, also called Lowton (GC) but it became Lowton St Mary's after nationalisation.

WEST OF KENYON JUNCTION, 1968. A Trans-Pennine unit is passing along the original Liverpool to Manchester line. In steam days, Black Fives and Royal Scot Classes hauled these trains as well as those from Liverpool to Newcastle. Dieselization with 2,000 hp Class 40s and ten coaches couldn't match the Trans-Pennine units and so, in the best traditions of BR marketing, one of the Stalybridge/Huddersfield stops was removed! So popular is this route now that it is to be electrified and to get new trains.

KENYON JUNCTION, 1952. Just under two miles east of Parkside is the junction of the line from Bolton at Kenyon Junction, formerly Bolton Junction until 1843. Extensive sidings were laid out as there were a number of collieries which fed onto the Bolton line. Shown looking north-east is the station which occupied an area totally out of proportion to the services it offered. Motor trains for Bolton (Great Moor Street), like the one shown, would continue for another two years with passenger services along the main line stopping six years later.

KENYON JUNCTION, 1954. Although nearer to Manchester (thirteen miles), than Liverpool (over eighteen miles), the station came under the latter's auspices for management, winning first prize in their Best Kept Station competition: an interesting concept in today's era. The main station buildings were on the Liverpool bound platform with an enormous covered footbridge joining it to the others. The style of the main building and canopy are similar to those at several stations along the L&M eg. Huyton, Rainhill and, with a variation, Earlestown.

KENYON JUNCTION, 1960. Class Five No. 44986, fitted with a self weighing tender, departs west from the sidings with a Parsonage Colliery (Leigh) to Warrington coal train in December. The domestic market was very important as most houses had coal fires and used Town Gas, made from coal; North Sea Gas, and central heating were not far away. A decline in demand and changes in production meant that the necessity for the junction ceased on 11 May 1969.

Seven
East of Wilderspool

The cessation of passenger services in 1962 from Liverpool to Manchester by way of Widnes, Warrington and Altrincham, marked the end of over 125 years of railway development involving four different railway companies. The first line went from St Helens to Runcorn Gap (Widnes) in 1832, followed by its extension west to Garston in 1852 and east to Warrington in 1853. The joint LNWR and MSLR line from Manchester's London Road to Broadheath, west of Altrincham, was soon followed by part of the Stockport to Warrington line, also in 1853. All of these came under the 'protective arm' of the LNWR in 1860, followed by the St Helens line four years later: the attempt of the company to look after its Liverpool-Manchester line meant that competition had to be absorbed.

EAST OF ARPLEY, 1966. On 12 February, Stanier 8F 2-8-0 No. 48495 is passing west with a fitted freight; after passing under the photographer it will pass over the River Mersey on a girder bridge. To its right is the Warrington bus depot and the sidings are actually the route of the original line to Manchester before the Ship Canal was built in 1893. Also on the right are sidings where coal was unloaded for Warrington Borough Council's electricity generating station. Coal went by conveyor belt under the track and the road and then across the River Mersey.

LATCHFORD, AROUND 1880. The station opened under the name of Latchford and Grappenhall until the completion of the line over the Manchester Canal on 9 August 1893. The level crossing next to the station and the one in the distance were typical of this route; in fact, one of the pieces of evidence against the withdrawal of passenger services in the early 1960s was that the boxes would still need to be manned for freight trains and so the savings would be minimal.

LATCHFORD, 1949. When the Manchester Ship Canal cut through the line a new route was required and constructed about 100 yards north. To give the 70-75 ft clearance necessary over the canal, the line went up at 1 in 93, passing over on what is locally known as the 'High Level Bridge'. In 1892 this was tested by the Board of Trade by having locos to the approximate weight of 750 tons driven onto it. This view is from the south bank of the canal. The station buildings of the closed station and its goods shed are the brick structures. Making up the back scene is the embankment carrying the new line. Just visible above the goods shed is the second station.

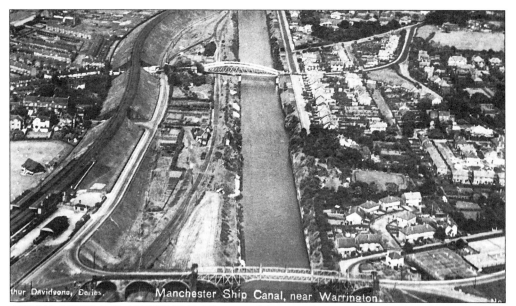

AERIAL VIEW OF LATCHFORD. The cut of the Manchester Ship Canal in this view to the east is prominent. Between the two bridges, on the left hand bank, are the lines that served the 'old' station which ran on the flat land, with the 'new' station in the bottom left corner. This line, and the CLC line near Partington, both had to be deviated and raised up to allow ships to pass under them. This gives some idea of the scale of not only the investment for the canal itself but also the associated infrastructure.

HIGH LEVEL BRIDGE, 1995. Even though passenger services ceased in 1962, the line carried a large amount of freight traffic, chiefly coal, to Fiddler's Ferry power station and oil tanks to refineries in the Wirral. In 1979 more than sixty trains a day were booked to pass across the bridge; many were subsequently diverted along different routes. However, since 7 July 1985, the through route has been severed by its closure. The critical factor was the heavy repairs that would have to be carried out, which was considered too much for about twenty of the trains that had to use it.

LATCHFORD STATION, EXTERIOR, BOOKING OFFICE. The booking office was at street level and of typical LNWR wooden construction. Steps led up to the platforms and there was a subway to the Manchester bound side.

LATCHFORD STATION, INTERIOR, BOOKING OFFICE. The interior of the booking office has its window festooned with awards and notices. The scene in a modern station appears different but is probably only tidier.

LATCHFORD, 1962. This was the view just before closure on 10 September. The LNWR prefabricated the buildings at its Crewe works, transported them to the site and erected them. They were without canopies and the platforms were also made of wood. The station had gas lights all its life.

LATCHFORD SIGNAL BOX. Situated just beyond the western end of the station, high above the houses, was this eighteen lever frame box. While it had a typical wooden cabin, the usual brick base was not used as was the case when there was the possibility of unstable ground, as here on the embankment.

LATCHFORD, 1962. A motor train has just arrived from Manchester: the driver was able to control the train by a series of cables and levers from the specially adapted end of a coach. The two signals on one post is an interesting economy measure. Pushing the train is Stanier 2-6-2T No. 41213. Typically, of the nine trains from Manchester stopping daily at Latchford, only two went the whole way to Liverpool. The majority went as far as Ditton Junction. Several services a day from St Helens also terminated there. Trains from Liverpool to Chester formed the connecting services. The line was seen very much as fourth fiddle to the trains between the two cities: the ex-L&M, the ex-L&Y and the ex-CLC lines all took precedence, although a fair amount of freight used it to relieve congestion on heavily used passenger lines.

WILDERSPOOL, 1890. Interestingly, the signal box was to the east of the crossing, by the steps to the footbridge. Old Road coal yard is also marked but not recorded photographically.

WILDERSPOOL CROSSING, 1961. Stanier 2-6-4T will have left Bank Quay Station a few minutes ago and has just passed the deserted platforms of Arpley Station. It is crossing the River Mersey and Wilderspool signal box is to the right. The alignment of the track illustrates the attention given to this, in passenger terms, backwater for fast trains.

WILDERSPOOL CROSSING, LOOKING SOUTH ABOUT 1900. This is a typical industrial street scene of almost 100 years ago. The building on the right is Latchford Wire Works with the signal cabin next to it: the wheel to control the gates can just be made out. On the left is the footbridge by the level crossing gates. In 1871 the Board of Trade recommended that a bridge be built here but locals baulked at the cost; it would take eighty-five years to achieve.

WILDERSPOOL CROSSING, 1954. This view looking north shows the level crossing and the adjacent footbridge. As this road was the main one south from Warrington, horrendous traffic congestion was caused each time the gates were closed. Soon the boarded up buildings would be demolished and replaced by a dual carriage way. The signal box is just visible on the left. A day out to Chester cost 2s 11d, or 15p in today's money.

Eight
Arpley and the West

Although Arpley was a joint station, it was misleading to think that passengers could travel directly to the company's namesakes. The Warrington & Stockport Railway only went as far as Altringham, where it met the LNWR and MSLR joint line to Manchester. To travel to St Helens in the west involved a change of trains at Widnes. How different would the area be if a regular, frequent rail service passed from Manchester via Stockport and Warrington to Liverpool? Instead of talking of closing the line due to maintenance of bridges, the environmental benefits of it would be the subject to discussion.

ARPLEY STATION, INTERIOR, 1957. For all its imposing exterior, there were only the two platform faces. This view looking east shows the extent of the passenger protection, the footbridge and the two other lines that separated the platforms. On the Manchester side was a loop, with two auto coaches on it, while on the Liverpool side, the line was a blind ending siding. During the electrification of the Liverpool to Crewe line in the late 1950s and early 1960s, Arpley was used as an alternative route. Trains would come down from the main line at Walton Junction. Another engine would be put onto what was the rear of the train, and off it would go, west to Liverpoool.

ARPLEY STATION, EXTERIOR, 1961. It opened on 1 May 1854 as a joint St Helens, and Warrington and Stockport, station. Prior to this, from 1 February 1853, the Warrington and Stockport had a temporary terminus at Wilderspool, to the east of the River Mersey. The St Helens Railway had had theirs to the west at Whitecross since 1 November 1853. The former company had their headquarters here, hence the rather imposing buildings. For some time there were two guns, captured in the Crimean War, in the large forecourt.

ARPLEY STATION, INTERIOR, 1890s. This view looks east with the goods shed in the foreground and the imposing station buildings in the middle. There was a large overall roof giving a good measure of passenger protection. A larger goods shed was to the south of the station; it is possibly a coal tank shunting wagons. The loco shed is off to the right.

MERSEY CROSSING, 1957. About to cross the bridge is ex-L&Y 0-6-0 No. 52225 on its way east. Until 1908 this bridge was tubular, similar to that at Menai, but with an open top. For many years the bridge carried an advertisement for 'Falstaff's Warrington Ale'. Just discernible across the Mersey is the new road bridge at Wilderspool. Ghost-like in the background is the electricity station, which, in the 1930s, supplied electricity at four units for an old penny!

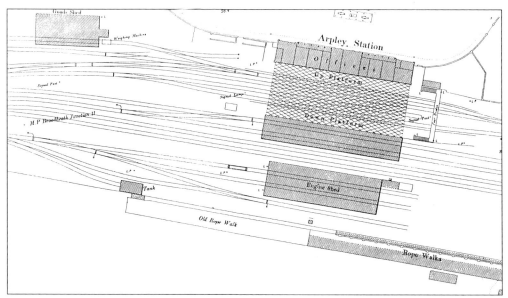

ARPLEY STATION 1888. This illustrates the overall roof from an aerial perspective. Apart from its removal, passengers noticed little other differences over the 100 years plus that the station was open.

ARPLEY STATION, 1961. A three coach push and pull train is being propelled west towards Bank Quay. Arpley Station actually closed twice. Having taken over the lines in the area, the LNWR raised their main line and built low level platforms where it passed over the former St Helens line; they then opened Bank Quay Station. On 16 November 1868, Arpley Station was closed as the company had no need of two stations on the same line, less than 500 yards apart. A local newspaper called the low level platforms, 'no more than a covered shed, open in front' with no separation for different classes.

ARPLEY STATION, 1963. The reputed 8,000 passengers per week who used Arpley forced the LNWR to think again and the company agreed to stop a few trains at Wilderspool Station, which had earlier closed, when Arpley opened. Due to the wording of the Act authorising the Warrington and Stockport Railway, the LNWR were forced, reluctantly, to re-open Arpley Station from 2 October 1871, so now they had an unnecessary station. It finally closed to passengers on 4 September 1958. Here Arpley is playing host to a RCTS Cheshire Rambler rail tour on 27 April, hauled by ex-LNER B1 Class 4-6-0 No. 61039 *Steinbok*.

ARPLEY SHED, 1963. The building to the right was a warehouse for Gartons, the seed merchants, showing its rail connections. On 27 April Fowler Class 4F locos Nos 44219 and 44589 are in residence.

ARPLEY SHED, 1936. A two road shed was developed, in the 1880s. To the left can be seen some sidings where the large shed was, with the Liverpool platform on the other side of the brick wall. It was unusual in that it was a through shed, with two arched doors. The roof, the biggest problem area for all sheds, still looks in good repair.

ARPLEY SHED, 1952. A study in 2-6-2 tank's rears. Stanier No. 41321 and Fowler 40042 stand outside the shed which looks in remarkably good condition, considering its age. This area is now the stabling point for diesels since the closure of Dallam Lane to steam in 1968.

ARPLEY SHED, INTERIOR, 1962. Inside the shed is 3F 0-6-0 No. 43240 on 17 June. The inspection pits and doors are plain to see, as is the almost complete absence of slates on the roof. When built it had smoke hoods and a central raised portion. Code 8B was Warrington (Dallam). Arpley, along with Over and Wharton, were sub sheds. It closed eleven months later.

ARPLEY JUNCTION, 1966. This view was taken from Slutcher's Lane Bridge, looking east, with the signal box and goods shed in the rear. Pushing an enthusiast's special train away from Arpley Station is Stanier 2-6-2T No. 41286. On the extreme right can be seen the remains of the turntable well. The junction was the meeting of the Warrington and Stockport branch to meet the Birkenhead, Lancashire and Cheshire Junction Railway line to Chester via Walton Junction (1856). This connection allowed GWR trains access to Manchester Exchange.

ARPLEY JUNCTION SIGNAL BOX. This is a typical LNWR structure: brick base with a wooden cabin on top. In 1996 it is still in use, as are the two sidings to the east of Wilderspool Causeway, the route of the original W&S line.

ARPLEY YARD, 1960. Birkenhead's Crab 2-6-0 No. 42942 pauses for water at the twin spouted tank with a freight train bound for Yorkshire. A magnificent example of a lattice post signal controls movements. Shunting in Arpley's sidings is an unidentified 0-6-0. Coal trains supply Fiddler's Ferry power station near Widnes. To get to it they pass down from Bank Quay (High Level) Station onto the joint GWR and LNWR line. A reversal takes place, through the site of Arpley Station and into the sidings mentioned above. At the allotted time they are hauled back through former Arpley and Bank Quay (Low Level) Stations, on their way west to the power station. The sidings to the right are also part of the complex that is part of today's freight network. Visible in the background are the tall semaphores controlling entrance to Bank Quay Station from the south.

SLUTCHERS LANE, 1957. This view looking east illustrates the twisting nature of the line: guaranteed to keep speeds low. The signal box was called Slutchers Lane and it replaced an earlier one on the other side of the line. The bridge leads to the Arpley Meadows industrial area and sidings, which were developed from 1900 between the branch from Arpley Junction and the LNWR main line over the Mersey.

WARRINGTON BANK QUAY, 1961. Opening on 16 November 1868, these platforms never had the official status of Low Level but did allow interchange between the north-south trains and the east-west ones: a modern transport planner's utopia! They were called platforms five and six. The canopy had ornate, curved iron supports and there was a covered footbridge. The wooden buildings are typical LNWR. Although closed to regular passengers in September 1962, it wasn't until three years later that it officially closed on 14 July 1965.

WARRINGTON BANK QUAY, 1962. Waiting in bay platform no. 7, is Stanier 2-6-2T No. 41211 with the 4.18 pm to Manchester on the last day of service, 8 September. Services like this stopped at all stations until the LNWR and MSLR joint line from Altrincham to Manchester was reached, then some of the suburban stations were missed; London Road's South Junction platforms were the terminal point. Crosfield's factories dominate the back scene.

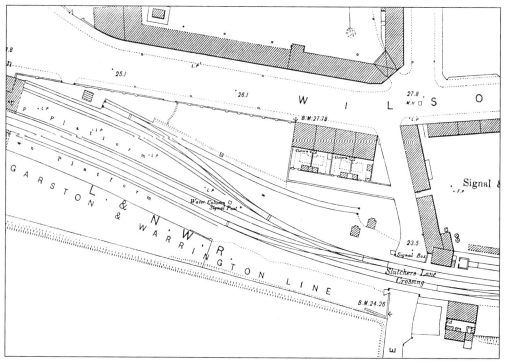

VIEW FROM SLUTCHER'S LANE BRIDGE, 1961. When looking at the same scene today, it is hard to imagine such a busy station ever existing. The signals are LNWR lower quadrants. The left hand train, being pushed by Standard Class No. 84000, is on its way to Ditton Junction. In the centre a train has just terminated a journey from Liverpool's Lime Street. Waiting in the bay platform is a sister LMS 2-6-2T before departing to Manchester's Oxford Road. In the background there is a Black Five passing through Bank Quay's high level platforms. Crosfield's transporter bridge stands out well.

Opposite: SLUTCHERS LANE, 1890. In railway infra-structure terms, very little, apart from the up sidings, has changed in the time between the map and the previous photograph. However, close examination shows that not only has the signal box changed sides, for sighting purposes presumably, but the crossing next to the dwellings has gone. It has been replaced by the bridge the photographer stood on.

LITTON'S MILL CROSSING, 1987. This LNWR type 3 (flush barge board and finial) box is where Quay Fold crosses the line to get to the mills between the line and the River Mersey. Its six levers control the semaphore signals that are very much alive and well. The pair visible protect Crosfield crossing, 200 yards to the east. The top arm is its home signal, while the lower arm belongs to the next one along the line, Slutchers Lane, some 450 yards away: a very congested area. Just to the east of the crossing was the site of Whitecross, the temporary terminus of the St Helens Railway from 1 February 1853 to 1 May 1854, until Arpley Station opened.

CROSFIELD'S CROSSING, 1987. Passengers standing on Bank Quay's platform four, looking west, can see the lines curving away beneath them and weaving between the towers of Lever's factories, once Crosfield's. In amongst the factories a public road crosses the line, protected by barriers and flashing lights. On their way to Fiddler's Ferry power station with one of the twenty-five daily train load of hoppers was a pair of diesel locos, Nos 20.041 leading 20.006, on 4 September. This small, eighteen lever box controls events.

MONKS SIDINGS, 1980. At the end of Beaufort Street, by the Coach and Horses pub, was the crossing to the iron and tube factories, south of the line but north of the Mersey. While a standard LNWR brick base with timber cabin and thirty levers, the hipped roof is different to the others along the line. The door and steps have been in at least two other places in this box! The main line passed in front of the box and the loops serving the factories were behind it, necessitating two lots of gates for the road. The steel works was that of Monks, Hall and Company.

SANKEY BRIDGES, 1950s. This station opened with the extension of the St Helens line east to Warrington on 1 February 1853. By this time, the canal and the railway were both owned by the St Helens Canal and Railway Company. To achieve the necessary clearance above the water the railway had to be on gentle gradients, 1 in 350 and 1 in 450. To provide more headroom would not only have cost more money in construction and maintenance, but also in the daily running expenses of the engines. The solution was to make a swing bridge.

SANKEY SWING BRIDGE, 1955. The rail bridge is open to allow barges to pass along the canal. At the time of opening, London trains from Liverpool along the line took a similar time to the LNWR's even though it needed an omnibus to transport passengers from the city centre to Garston. This was due to the LNWR still using the winding engines at Lime Street and the sharp curves at Earlestown. The swing bridge was used for traffic until the 1950s. Although the station closed in 1949 the line is still in use today for freight.

RISLEY. West of Glazebrook the line passed over Risley Moss, a southern extension of the famous Chat Moss that needed special features to be employed in the building of the L&M in the 1830s. For this section of line the land was extensively drained before construction began. A temporary station was opened in the Second World War, on 2 April 1940, to serve an adjacent ordnance factory. In a dilapidated state it closed on 6 April 1964. In the 1970s however, a housing development was located on the site of the former factory and a new station, Birchwood, opened on 6 October 1980, a short distance west of Risley.

PADGATE, c. 1920. This station was practically identical to Glazebrook and opened at the same time. The main buildings are on the Manchester side. Originally there were steps down from the over bridge to each platform and there are well used sidings, on both up and down sides. In the late 1960s the goods yard and sidings closed, but the basic buildings are still in good repair. North of the line at Padgate, sidings were laid as headquarters for a ballast train. A shed was also built for the loco that hauled the train over the entire CLC system from Southport to Chester until the mid 1930s.

PADGATE JUNCTION. In the 1865 Act, the plan was to build Warrington's station on the Straight Line, but due to public pressure, powers were obtained the next year for the construction of a loop that passed through the centre of the town: the avoiding line was deferred. When it was first built the line went from Padgate Station south to Warrington, and then north to Sankey. Some ten years later – 13 August 1883 for goods, 7 September for passengers – the Straight Line, an avoiding line for Warrington, was built between Padgate and Sankey. This view east shows GCR B7 4-6-0 No. 5037 pulling a freight train on the just over two mile avoiding line in pre grouping days.

PADGATE JUNCTION. Passing the controlling signal box is GCR 4-4-0 No. 1016 in the early part of this century. In 1951 those passenger trains passing along the avoiding line went from city to city in forty-five minutes, just five minutes longer than before the First World War. The stop at Warrington added five more minutes to the journey time.

PADGATE   JUNCTION

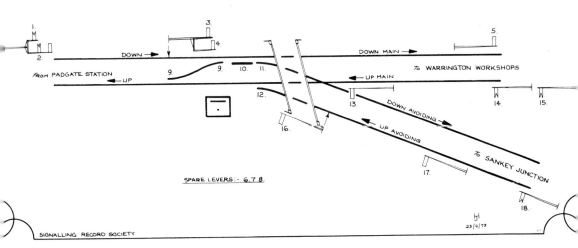

SIGNAL BOX DIAGRAM, PADGATE JUNCTION. As much signalling on today's system is by electric colour lights, it is not as obvious to the travelling public as semaphores were. The above diagram illustrates that the industry had gone a long way since the 1830s. Then, signals, were exhibited by policemen (Bobbies) who were also expected to preserve order at stations. As the latter became longer, a person in charge was appointed, called a 'pointsman' or 'signalman'. There are many pubs close to junctions with these names. It was an obvious development to provide a separate building for such people: it encouraged concentration on the job, making for a more efficient system. The whole operation became too complex for people to operate satisfactorily so the development of the interlocking of points and signals took off. During 1863 the firm of Saxby and Farmer built a larger new works beside the main line at Kilburn and produced many frames for differnet railway companies. Adjacent signal boxes communicated with each other by a special code of bells, and passed this message on to the train driver using the signals. In this way, a smooth flow according to the timetable was ensured. (Diagram by courtesy of the Signalling Railway Society)

WARRINGTON CENTRAL, EXTERIOR, 1982. This was an impressive station compared to the others on the line, as befitting a town the size of Warrington. These are the station buildings on the north (Manchester) side of the station. By 1982 these impressive buildings had been closed for some years and a more 'public friendly' entrance and facilities had been opened from Winwick Street. Thankfully, a public relations firm took over the old buildings and so they still stand.

WARRINGTON CENTRAL, 1959. A meeting of the trains between the two largest cities in Lancashire. Arriving from Manchester is Stanier 2-6-4T No. 42612, while having arrived from Liverpool is smaller sister engine No. 40094. For a few years from 1875, the Midland Railway operated a Pullman service from Liverpool, via Warrington and Manchester, to St Pancras. Its timing was competitive to the LNWR's as they were still rope hauling trains from Lime Street to Edge Hill.

WARRINGTON CENTRAL, INTERIOR, 1961. The station was re-roofed with the saw toothed canopy being replaced by this flat glazed one; the fancy iron work is gaily painted. In 1910 the fast trains left Warrington for Liverpool taking twenty-five minutes, and for Manchester taking twenty minutes: times little changed since inception in 1877 with the opening of Manchester Central Station. Forty years and two World Wars later, the journeys would both have been accomplished in a time five minutes longer.

WARRINGTON CENTRAL, 1955. About to depart east is Class D11/1 4-4-0 No. 62668 *Jutland* on 28 August. The trains along the CLC route had built up a reputation as the 'punctual' service in competition with the LMS routes, the ex-L&M from Exchange via Earlestown, the ex-L&Y from Victoria. The few through trains belonging to a variety of former owners through southern Warrington's, Arpley and Bank Quay Stations, were hardly a contender for such passengers.

125

WARRINGTON GOODS SHED, 1981. To the north east of the station were extensive sidings and this impressive 200 ft by 50 ft goods shed, which is still standing in 1996. The end panels were inscribed with the name of the amalgamated company and the date, 1897. The names of the three constituent companies, as well as the combined company, were written on the four northern panels facing the station. To the east were the CLC's Battersby Lane workshops for signals, some rolling stock repair and from 1886, their tickets. As a joint railway the company had everything except locomotives. In post grouping times, 1923-1947, different jobs went to different parts of the parent companies, making it a bureaucratic nightmare to operate. The other large joint railway, Midland and Great Northern, also had locos.

WARRINGTON SIGNAL BOX, 1982. On the same site as the 1883 structure it replaced, is this modern wooden box controlling colour lights which replaced the fine semaphores seen in other pictures.

WARRINGTON LOCO SHED, 1960. To call this a shed is rather a misnomer: it is more like a stabling point. To the right of this view is a wall with the Liverpool platform behind it; to the left it is quite a drop to Crown Street. Here a LMS 4F 0-6-0 is awaiting its next trip. In earlier years, some distance to the west, there was a turntable on the branch which served the Whitecross Wire and Iron works.

Acknowledgements

This book was born out of the desire to unravel the complex railway network in the heartland of industrial Lancashire. No book is the sole work of one person and this one is no exception. Its existence is due to persistent research, supported by local people. Without the support of local history libraries and societies in the three major towns, it wouldn't have been possible. I am particularly indebted to residents Graham Earl in Widnes, Dave Forrest in Warrington and Mary Presland in St Helens. I thank them for all their advice, encouragement and help. Special mention must be made of Eddie Bellas, who besides letting me use numerous photographs, also provided valuable background information.

Many people have lent me materials and photographs; I hope I have listed them all and apologise in advance for any omissions. As in any historical document, there will be different opinions about the importance and relevance of evidence. Some data is different depending on the source, therefore the desire for accuracy continues and if anyone can substantiate or correct a point, I would be only too pleased to hear from them.

Thanks to: K. Oldham, N. Preedy, M.A. King, N.D. Mundy, I.G. Holt, H.C. Casserley, J. Peden, C. Dixon, R.H. Robinson, D. Skipsey, J, Gregory, D. Butterfield and N. Stead, R.K. Blencowe, P. Hutchinson, G.B. Ellis, L. Hanson, R.H. Brough, R.S. Carpenter, H.B. Priestly, R. Morten, C. Townley, N. Frazer, R. Humm, L. Vaughan, J. Townley, D. Forrestt, N. Brooksbank, G. Earl, J. Ryan, B. Morrisson, J. Sommerfield, F. Dean, M.H. Walshaw, P. Norton, Stations UK, A.K. Jones collection, British Waterways, R. Humm, Historical Model Railway Society, Lancashire and Yorkshire Railway Society, London and North Western Railway Society, Great Central Railway Society, Signalling Recording Society, Rail and Canal Historical Society, Mowat Collection, Warrington, Widnes and St Helens Libraries, National Monuments Record Centre.

In today's market place a great number of photographs are for sale: some are copies of originals without the owner's knowledge or permission. If, in this book, there is a picture from your collection and I haven't credited you, I apologise.